lorraine osborne

THE STUFF

upholstery, fabric, frame.

SCHIFFER
PUBLISHING

4880 Lower Valley Road • Atglen, PA 19310

Photography Credits
The Really Good Media Company
Front cover, and pages 2, 5, 10, 12, 25 bottom, 26/27, 42 all images, 43 middle and bottom right, 51, 52, 65 top right and bottom, 66, 78, 82, 89 bottom right and bottom middle, 90, 91, 94, 96/97, 104/105, 110/111, middle right, 112/113, 116 images 12 - 15, 117 all images, 132, 145 middle, 160, 161, 168, 170, 171.
Page 99 top right, Diego Azubel/EPA/Shutterstock.
Pages 6, 82, 96, 103 Getty.
Page 86 bottom left, 99 bottom middle, Boston Globe/Getty.]
Page 68 Bob Razzer.
Every effort has been made to contact the copyright holders of the images in this book. But should there be any errors or omissions, the publisher would be pleased to insert the appropriate acknowledgement in any subsequent printing of this book.

All other photography Lorraine Osborne

Library of Congress Control Number: 2020952428

Produced by BlueRed Press Ltd, 2021
Designed by Insight Design Concepts Ltd.
Type set in Gotham

ISBN: 978-0-7643-6303-0
Printed in India

Published by Schiffer Publishing, Ltd.
4880 Lower Valley Road
Atglen, PA 19310
Phone: (610) 593-1777; Fax: (610) 593-2002
Email: Info@schifferbooks.com
Web: www.schifferbooks.com

For our complete selection of fine books on this and related subjects, please visit our website at www.schifferbooks.com. You may also write for a free catalog.

Schiffer Publishing's titles are available at special discounts for bulk purchases for sales promotions or premiums. Special editions, including personalized covers, corporate imprints, and excerpts, can be created in large quantities for special needs. For more information, contact the publisher.

We are always looking for people to write books on new and related subjects. If you have an idea for a book, please contact us at proposals@schifferbooks.com.

The Little Upholstery Book: A Beginner's Guide to Artisan Upholstery, Shelly Miller Leer, ISBN 978-0-7643-5742-8

Upholstery: Basic & Traditional Techniques, Santiago Pons, Eva Pascual, Jordi Pons & Mercè Garcinuño, 978-0-7643-4855-6

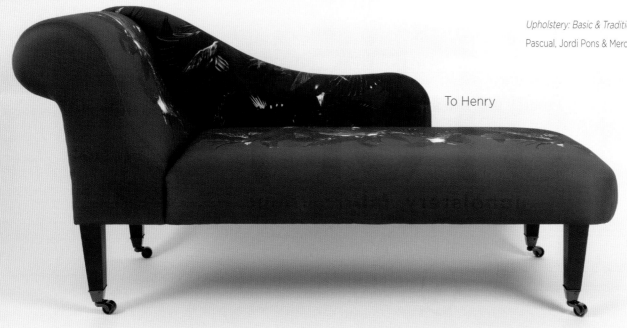

To Henry

contents

the yarn
why me?

I'm a traditionally trained upholsterer by trade—and have been since way back in the mid-1980s. These days I make the furniture I want to make. It's modern in construction and tends to reflect who I am and what I love (or hate) about the world. Actually, whatever is going on my head will sooner or later end up as a design on a chair—you could say upholstery has become my art.

I have two ambitions for this book. First, I hope to influence the way you choose the chairs that you renovate. It saddens me to see the treasures that end up in the non recycle skip at our local refuse depot.

Far too much modern furniture is thrown away—and with it the perfectly good materials and resources it contains that ought to be reused. Mass-produced chairs have been shamefully wasted for years and it's time we changed that.

It's not the furniture that's lacking—it's our imaginations.

Secondly I would love to share with you the joy of unrolling your first fabric design. I've printed miles of fabric over the years and yet I still get stupidly excited to see how my latest creation has turned out.

These days there are plenty of software programs available to the amateur fabric designer; most of them will offer you a free trail—some are free to download. (*See* the fabric/designing chapter). I taught myself how to put my designs on fabric using the Photoshop design program on my laptop and an online fabric printing service; I promise you, I was barely computer literate when I started.

In preparation for the book, I thought I ought to do a course and load up on expertise and jargon, but I decided that it would be unfair to present myself as an expert when all the fabric in this book was produced without the benefit of formal education. So, what you have here is most definitely a beginner's guide to digital fabric design.

I can't save all the chairs —I need your help!

This isn't, however, a beginner's guide to upholstery. The last time I looked online there were over fifty of those titles and countless upholstery tutorials. That base is well and truly covered. The only processes, therefore, that I am going to explain step-by-step, are my own very simple techniques. I promise you don't have to be a master craftsman or a tech head to get the best outcome with your own designs.

What you do need are a few basic upholstery skills, an ability to work three-dimensionally, and an eye for shape and design—plus what my mum would call "a bit of flair."

I sincerely hope my work will inspire you to think more creatively about the chairs you choose to reinvent, and encourage you to develop a style and a voice of your own.

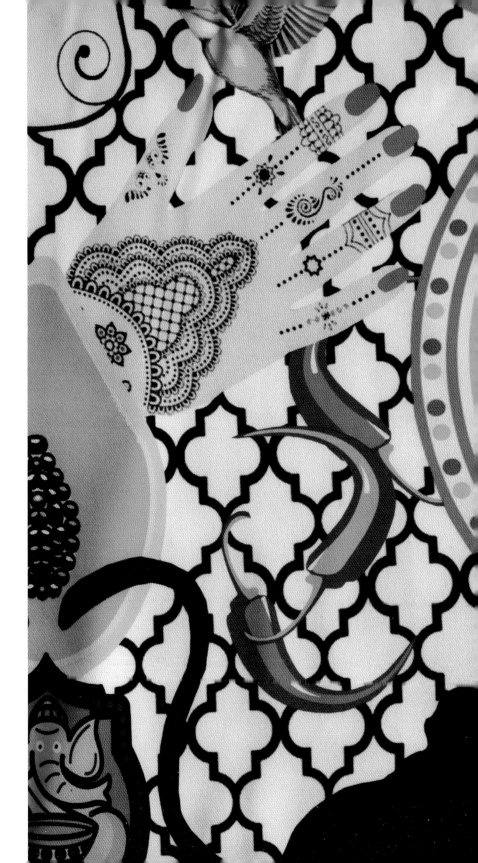

the idea

inspiration

I doubt if I can say anything particularly insightful or new about inspiration—we all know how it feels to be inspired and what a fantastic feeling that is! What inspires me are the ordinary things I see in my everyday life—a colony of microbes in a petri dish, an old-school tattoo, or some lovely ovaries. (1)

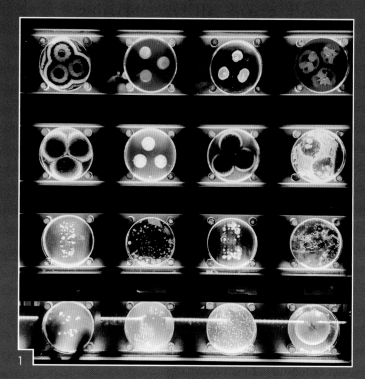

1

People inspire my designs too: women in particular. The heavy lifters who have made life easier for my daughter and me, especially if the extraordinary things they have done have gone uncelebrated or not celebrated enough. Take, for example, nineteen-year old Florence Ilott, who was working as a waitress at the House of Commons Tea Room in the 1930s. There's an ancient tradition among the men who work at the Houses of Parliament to attempt to run across Westminster Bridge within the twelve chimes of noon. Florence nipped out in her lunch break and caused a sensation by becoming the first person on record to achieve this. I have featured her story along with five other outstanding runners on a three-panel screen for International Women's Day. (2, 3)

2

3

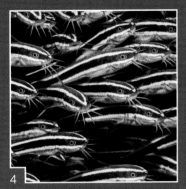

4

5

The natural world is another infinite source of inspiration, of course. Just when I think the world can't get any more beautiful, along comes the image of a writhing bed of black and white catfish eels and suddenly my heart is beating a little faster. Nailing those critters in a design may be difficult and frustrating, but that's what makes it so satisfying. (4, 5)

message

Personally, I think it's fun to write messages on furniture: my customers seem to like it and it keeps me away from Twitter. If I have a point to make, I do my best to get it across with subtlety and wit. It's never my intention to harangue the public with my opinions—more like a tongue-in-cheek dig in the ribs.
I hope my scribbling will inspire you to create fabric that expresses whatever it is that you are passionate about. Subtly, of course. (6)

love

If your design doesn't make your heart sing, chances are it won't make anyone else's heart sing either. Perhaps the shape isn't particularly sexy, or the black and white catfish eel design didn't turn out how you imagined. Whatever it is—stop and have a rethink.
The world is full of chairs that were made with competence and good intentions but no love. You have to love your chair!

6

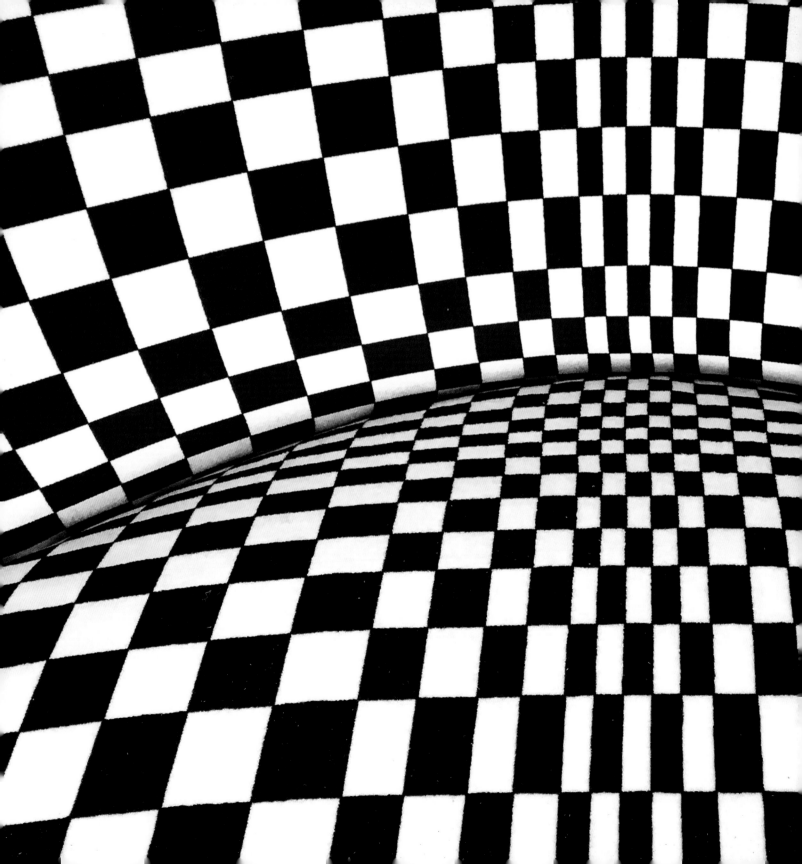

the stuff

lovely ovaries

Someone I love very much invited me to sit
in on their scan. Big mistake.

As the technician was doing his thing with
the scanner and watching the monitor he
said, sotto voce, almost to himself, "Lovely
ovaries . . ."

I could see what he meant—they were lovely.

I later discovered that the illustrated cross
section of an ovary contains a garden of
wonderful things that look like flowers and
ribbons and shiny strings of beads.
So I decided to present an ovary as a
luscious bountiful fruit—a tea table full of
delights.

Once I had discovered that the anatomical contents of an ovary included jam tarts and tiny fried eggs there was no going back.

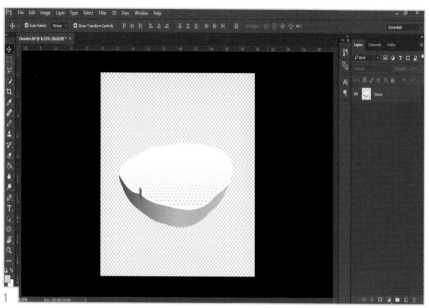

1

The Fabric
Photoshop
The *lovely ovaries* fabric

I began by downloading the image of a cross-sectioned ovary from the internet. My plan was to simplify the image to look like a fruit cut in half, with a tea table inside.

I downloaded an image of pale gray stars for the tablecloth, and an image of a mango for the bottom half of the ovary. Using Photoshop, I took the Pen tool and cropped out the shape of the top of the ovary. Then, using the Move tool, I dragged the whole image (with a hole in the middle shaped like the top of the ovary) onto the image of pale gray stars.

I merged the two layers.

Then I cropped out the bottom half of the ovary and dragged the whole image (this time with a bottom-shaped hole in the middle) onto the image of a mango. I merged these layers too.

Now the stars and the mango were fixed as the top and bottom of the ovary. I then cropped out the whole ovary and dragged it onto a new canvas 8in x 8in (20.5cm x 20.5cm)/1181px x 1181px/150dpi (dots per inch), and called it Ovaries.

This gave the bottom of the ovary a lovely fruity color while the top of the ovary had a crisp, white, star-studded tablecloth. No doubt there are cleverer ways of doing this, but this is how I did it for my design. (1)

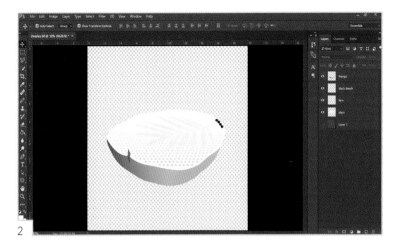

2

3

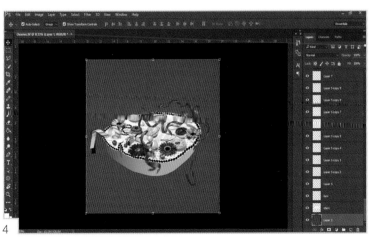

4

Now the Fun Begins

I aimed to replicate the objects in the anatomical illustration as closely as possible with everyday things such as beads, ribbons, daisies, and doughnuts. So I sourced suitable images online and cropped, dragged, and dropped them onto the tablecloth.

When I made this design I had just taught myself how to put a shadow under an object. As you can see from the list of layers, everything has a shadow! (*See* the fabric/*I'm Not Here!* exercise.)

I had also begun to try different background colors against the ovary design: my original thought was arsenic or leaf green. In view of the anatomical nature of the design, I thought it best to stay away from red, and yet it turned out to be the perfect complement to the design. I tried out a few different shades, but in the end I settled on a warm earthy red that was borrowed from an image of dried paprika.

I used the Set foreground color and Eyedropper tools to sample the color from a downloaded image of paprika, and the Paint pot tool to change the background. (2, 3, 4)

PROJECT lovely ovaries

Once I was happy with the spread of lovely things on the tea table, I merged all layers into one ovary image. Then I put a shadow under the ovary on a separate layer. Finally, I saved the file as a TIFF to keep the layers separate. This way I could drag the ovary onto a new background and reposition the shadow if necessary. (5)

I was extremely pleased with the ovary, but I thought the image wasn't enough on its own. It needed something interesting floating around in the background. Babies ... obviously.

Background Babies

I downloaded an image of a baby and, using the digital pen, drew a solid black line around the shape. Then I cropped out the shape and dragged it to a new canvas sized 8in x 8in (20 x 20cm)/1181px x 1181px/150dpi.

Using the Magic eraser tool I got rid of everything inside the shape, so I was left with a clear outline of a baby. I have to go through this rigmarole because I can't draw—hopefully you will be able to just draw whatever you want and get on with it!

I colored the baby's skin by using the Set foreground color/Eyedropper/Paint pot tools. Then I drew on a white diaper (I just about managed that) using the digital pen. I gave her big shiny eyes, a nose, a mouth, and the suspicion of a dimple—also using the digital pen.

5

I added a new layer under the baby for the background color of paprika red. Then, on another new layer, gave her a deep shadow as though the sun were shining brightly overhead. I saved the file as a TIFF (to keep the layers separate) and made a copy. (6)

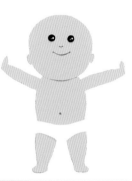

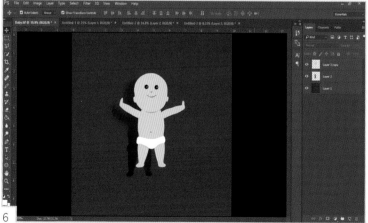

6

7

Now I had to turn the baby into a repeatable background fabric. I wanted every other baby to be upside down (and upside-down babies need upside-down shadows). I opened the copy of the Baby.tif and flipped the image upside down. Then I deleted the existing shadow and replaced it with an appropriate shadow. I flattened the layers in both the original file and the upside-down copy and saved them as Baby.jpg and Baby 1.jpg (7)

All I had to do now was bring the two elements of my design together. I chose to print my design on 59in (150cm) wide Panama heavy cotton, which is a smooth, densely woven cotton that faithfully replicates detailed designs: I wanted to see every raspberry and dimple.

I made a new canvas that was half the width of the fabric—29.5in x 12in (75cm x 30cm)—and deep enough to fit the ovary motif comfortably. I dragged Baby.jpg and Baby 1.jpg onto the canvas and duplicated them in a brick pattern until I had three rows of babies.

Using the Offset tool, I made sure the design would repeat horizontally. I saved a copy of the baby background and called it Babies.jpg. Then I went back to the Ovary.tif and dragged the ovary image onto the baby background. Then I dragged the shadow layer onto the background (under the ovary layer). I did this twice

to get two ovaries and their shadows positioned perfectly side by side.

This gave me an idea of the overall look of the fabric. I flattened the layers and saved the image as Lovely Ovaries.jpg. The file was ready to upload to the printer. (8)

8

PROJECT lovely ovaries

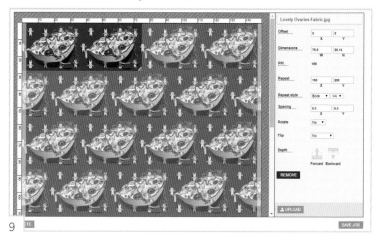

I already had the chair I was going to use for the project. It was tiny and needed only about 10ft (3m) of fabric in total. (*See* fabric/quantifying.)

However, I was beginning to think that the lovely ovaries fabric would make more of an impact if I used it to cover the inside back and seat only. The floating babies would make a very cute companion fabric to cover the seat panel/back panel and outside back. So I uploaded the Lovely Ovaries.jpg to the online fabric printers and ordered just 6.5ft (2m) of Panama heavy cotton. (9)

The Babies Fabric

I went back to the copy of Babies.jpg and dragged it onto a new canvas sized 16in x 16in (40cm x 40cm)/2362px x 2362px/150dpi. The Lovely Ovaries.jpg file was 29.5in (75cm) wide—half the width of the fabric, 59in (150cm). The new canvas was roughly a quarter of the width, so would scale down the design by a quarter.

I duplicated the babies vertically until I had filled the new square canvas. Finally, I saved the image as Babies Fabric.jpg, uploaded it to the online printers, and ordered 39in (1m) of Panama heavy cotton. (10, 11, 12)

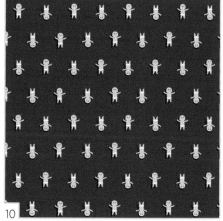

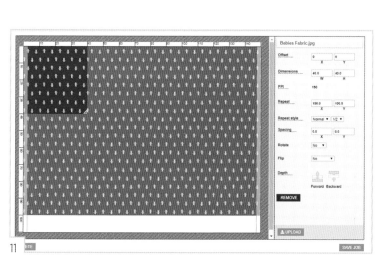

The Chair

I've bought several little mid-century chairs like this—they seem to have rather a lot of them in eastern Europe. They pop up quite often on eBay, very cheap, but you have to be patient until they sell enough of them to fill up a van and drive to the UK. I'm lucky to live in a beautiful part of rural Devon, so by the time the charming east European drivers get to my workshop they have been lost for hours and are resigned to the idea of a nice day out in the countryside. (13)

First, I unbolted the arms and put the bolts in an envelope that I pinned to my workshop noticeboard, clearly marked "Ovaries." Be careful not to lose anything you unscrew from a frame; it can be really difficult to replace old fittings—and such a nuisance.

I had hoped to sand down the frame and simply put a couple of coats of clear wax on the warm honey-colored show wood, but unfortunately the arms were quite stained around the bolts. This is often the case with furniture that has been exposed to the elements. Plan B was to give the frame my usual black paint treatment, which turned out for the best—the wood looked really sharp in black. I painted the frame just before the polyester went on.
(*See* the frame/finishing.)

Sadly I couldn't leave any of the original upholstery in place and only the old top cover could be recycled for rags. (14)

13

14

15

16

17

Foam

I started by webbing the seat and inside back, then stapling a layer of tarpaulin (or heavy hessian) over the webbing to make a platform for the new foam. (15)

I began by building up the seat with layers of 0.6in (1.5cm) blue (firm seating) foam. First, I marked the middle of the frame at the front and back of the seat. Then I drew a line with a marker pen down the center of each piece of cut foam. I carefully matched the center line of the foam to the center marks on the chair, then glued each layer in place using plenty of spray adhesive on both surfaces.

Each layer that I added was cut a little longer at the front to form a pointed edge to the foam (echoing the pointed edge at the front of the frame). I could have used layers of 0.8in (2cm) foam but I prefer to build up the shape on a little chair like this with thin layers. I glued two narrow strips of foam along the front edge (one slightly deeper than the other) to soften the shape. Then I glued a single piece of 0.6in (1.5cm) foam over the seat and front edge to finish. (16)

I cut out two 0.6in (1.5cm) foam shapes to make the bottom panels at the side of the seat by drawing around the new profile of the seat. These bottom panels were glued in place first, then the cut edges were glued together, then I glued a strip of polyester along the join to hold everything in place. I also cut a hole in the foam where the arm would be bolted back on the frame. (17)

The inside back was built up in a similar process to the seat. This time I glued just two layers of 0.6in (1.5cm) foam under the top layer of foam; the top layer covered the whole of the inside back and top edge (matching center lines at the top and bottom of the inside back) and just a single strip was added to the top edge to soften the shape. I filled in the top panels in the same way as the bottom panels—remembering to cut a little hole in the foam where the arm would be bolted back on the frame. (18, 19)

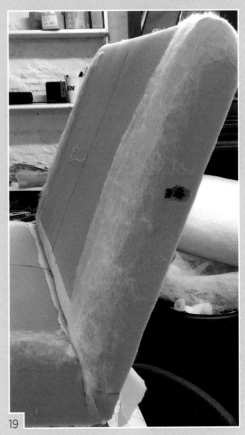

Template

Now I was ready to make a calico template to use as a pattern to cut the top fabric. When making a template, symmetry is everything. So check that the center lines on the inside back and seat foam are straight and centered before starting. You only ever make a template of one half of the chair, so if the lines aren't in the middle, the cover won't fit!

I began by measuring out a rectangle of calico big enough to make the inside back and seat in one piece, plus a 3in (8cm) gully (tuck-in) where the inside back meets the back of the seat.

Note: Calico is a loomstate fabric, which means it is sold as it comes off the loom and can look a bit wonky. To cut out a true (straight) piece of calico you have to measure out what you want, snip with the scissors, and tear the fabric along the grain. It will still look wonky, but it will be "true."

I folded the calico piece in half lengthways and snipped a tiny triangular notch to mark the center, top, and bottom. Then I drew a line in ballpoint pen from notch to notch down the center. I matched the centerline on the calico to the centerlines on the inside back and seat foam and tucked in the 3in (8cm) I had allowed for the gully. A few anchoring pins held the calico in place on the chair. (20)

I cut out two pieces of calico big enough to cover the bottom panel and the top panel, plus a generous allowance (1.9in/5cm) for pinning, which will be trimmed to 0.6in (1.5cm) and put them both in place with a few anchoring pins. I temporary-tacked the edges of the template to the frame to add a little more stability while I was pinning the seams. Then I pinned together the new seams around the bottom and top panels.

> *Note: When you pin a shape like this, it's important to check regularly that the seams you are making look straight from the front as well as the side. They can very easily go off the rails if you stand only at the side of the chair.*

Also at this point I clearly labeled each calico pattern piece, inside back/seat/top panel/bottom panel, and I drew an arrow pointing to the top of the chair at right angles to the floor. This will help keep the design straight when I cut out the fabric—especially on the top panel, which is sloping backward. Finally, I pushed a ballpoint pen down the back of the seat and drew a line across the bottom of the 3in (8cm) gully. I will cut along this line to separate the inside back and seat pieces. This will enable me to lay the pattern pieces in two places to match the fabric. I also drew two lines marking where the inside back and the seat came together on the chair. I will also use these two lines to pattern-match the fabric. (21, 22)

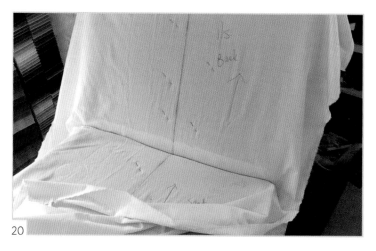

20

21

22

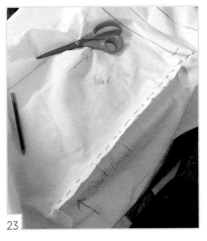

23

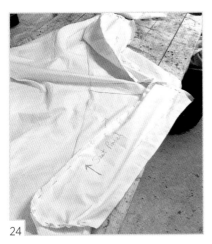

24

25

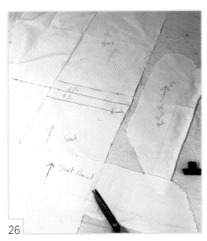

26

27

28

I always take my time pinning and repinning a template until it's perfect. It's well worth all the effort when the pattern pieces of the top fabric are sewn together and they slide onto the chair and fit! When I was happy with the seams, I took out the anchoring pins (not the seam pins) and temporary tacks and carefully took the template off the chair. I trimmed the pinned seams down to 0.6in (1.5cm) all the way around, and snipped in tiny random notches. (23, 24)

Then I took out all the seam pins. The inside back/seat piece of the pattern was folded down the centerline and laid on the table. A few pins held it in place while I cut around the shape to make a mirror image (not forgetting to cut the tiny notches). Finally, I cut the inside back/seat pattern piece in half along the gully line. Now the template was complete.
I had four beautiful pattern pieces: inside back, seat, bottom panel, and top panel. (25, 26)

Polyester
There's a lot of spray adhesive flying around at the polyester stage, so if the weather is not wet or windy I recommend that you take your chair outside to avoid breathing in the fumes.

First, where the inside back meets the seat, I glued two panels of calico to the foam: one attached to the inside back, one attached to the seat. This helps the polyester slide through the gap and not stick to the foam. (27, 28)

Then I glued two layers of polyester down the center of the inside back and seat to create a slightly domed effect and offset the flatness of the new foam. The middle section of the top panel and bottom panel also needed building up; I glued three strips of polyester in the center of each panel (but not on the edge). (29, 30)

One final layer of polyester was glued to the inside back, seat, top panel, and bottom panel. Then, following the same lines as the foam joins underneath, the polyester pieces are glued and pressed together (like crimping a pie or pasty). When the glue was dry I trimmed the seams. This method of fixing the polyester layers will keep everything where it's supposed to be when I pull the top cover tightly over the top. Last, I trimmed the polyester away from the arm bolt holes. (31, 32)

Cutting the Fabric

First, I laid my gorgeous fabric on the table and had a good look at the overall design before cutting. I had printed the fabric in a quarter-brick repeat pattern, so the ovaries ran diagonally across the width. I was using only the *lovely ovaries* fabric on the inside back and seat, so it was important to get an exact pattern match where these two pieces came together—this is where all those careful lines come in!

The calico template for the inside back and seat was made in one piece and cut along the line that I drew at the bottom of the gully

(tuck in). Now that the pattern pieces were separate I could lay them in two different places on the fabric. As well as the gully line I had drawn two lines on the calico pattern marking where the inside back came together with the seat; now I was able to use these lines to find the pattern match.

Once the two pieces were in place on the fabric, I added a 0.6in (1.5cm) seam allowance to the bottom of the inside back and the top of the seat. This would enable me to machine-sew the gully back together. I pinned the pattern pieces in place and had one last check before I cut them out, not forgetting to cut the notches. (33, 34)

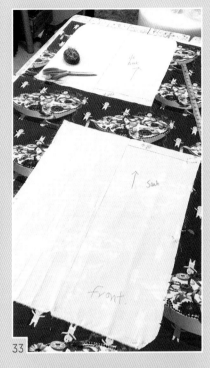

33

34

35

36

Then I laid out the babies fabric to cut the top and bottom panels. Keeping the arrows straight and trying to avoid too many decapitated babies, I placed, pinned, and cut out the left panels.

Then, using the two cut out left-hand panels as pattern pieces, I pinned them on the same part of the pattern and cut out the right-hand panels. This way the baby pattern was the same on both sides of the chair. (35, 36)

It was time to put this lovely top cover together. First, I pinned (matching center notches) and machined the gully seam between the inside back and the seat. Then, matching notches, I pinned and machined the short diagonal seam connecting the top panel to the bottom panel. Next the two long seams attaching the inside back to the top panel and the seat to the bottom panel were carefully matched, pinned, and machined. Once I have a piece of sewing like this assembled, I usually whiz the seams through the sewing machine again for added strength. Finally, I machined a panel of calico to the gully seam allowance. Once the top cover was in place on the chair I'd pull this calico panel through the gap between the inside back and seat and staple it to the frame.

Now that the sewing was complete I slid the cover onto the chair, making sure that the center notches on the cover matched up with the center marks on the chair. I started by temporary-tacking the cover in place. I pulled through the calico panel that was sewn to the gully seam and temporary-tacked it to the seat rail at the back of the chair, pulling the fabric to the bottom of the gully. (37, 38)

Where the inside back panel was joined to the seat panel, I made a diagonal fold and temporary-tacked the end of the fold to the back of the frame. Then I made two V-shaped cuts around the front legs, and two corner cuts around the back legs, and temporary-tacked the cover to the underside of the frame. (39)

When everything was looking good I stapled the cover to the frame. Now for the really scary bit. In order to bolt the arms back in place I had to make bolt holes in the perfect top cover.
I carefully felt for the holes and made tiny crosscuts for the bolts to go through. Nerve-racking stuff! (40)

I blocked in the outside back cavity with calico, but any strong cloth that you have spare will do the job. Because the back legs were covering the rail at the bottom of the outside back I had to machine-sew the outside back fabric to the black base cloth (the seam sat in the narrow gap under the back legs). First I pinned, then nailed the outside back fabric in place with black-headed gimp pins (fine upholstery pins) and

attached the black base cloth with tacks. (41, 42, 43)

To finish, I usually nail a woven name label to the base cloth. (44)

Here's a beautiful, labyrinthine thought. A female foetus has about two million eggs in her ovaries. If a mother is expecting a baby girl she is carrying her grandchildren, too.

39

Calico panel
37

40

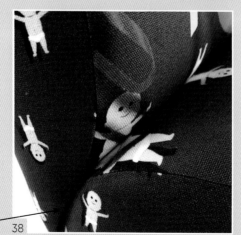
Gully stops here
38

41

42

43

44

drawing blood

I'm obsessed with my health and longevity and plan to live to at least 120. I don't smoke, and barely drink. I eat a very carefully sourced plant-based diet, take handfuls of supplements, and exercise daily.

I'm unbearable.

Last year I consulted a functional medicine doctor and had an extensive blood test to see how well I was doing; cholesterol, thyroid, liver function, inflammation, blood counts—the lot.

The results were so resoundingly vindicating I just had to print my diet all over a large chair for everyone to see.

Sorry kids—see you in 2081 if you make it.

blue green algae, Spirulina, contains vitamins A, C, E & B. Plus tons of minerals
sweet corn parsnips quinoa tea chocolate
garlic capers sardines olives chick peas
cauliflower yeast extract walnuts globe artichoke pear
help anxiety and depression and can calm you down at bed-time.
miso sage red lentils parsley basil green tea rice swede
Pink Himalayan Salt contains more calcium, potassium, magnesium and iron then regular Salt.
Garlic contains anti-oxidants that protect against cell damage and aging.
Breathing lavender oil focuses the mind and helps the memory.
beans and whole grains for copper.
Zinc helps
walnuts beetroot
P
Phosphorus
30.974
Mn
Manganese
54.938
Zn
Zinc
126.904

PROJECT drawing blood

1

2

The Fabric

It wasn't going to be easy distilling so much vital information onto a fabric design, but tree trunks and blood-vessel branches seemed a good place to start. My design could evolve from there.

Photoshop

I went online and found a simple seamless image of tree trunks and downloaded it. Then I dragged the image onto a new canvas sized 8 x 8in (20 x 20cm)/1181 x 1181px/150dpi. (1)

I changed the background to a color close to the famous Yves Saint Laurent inky blue, using the Set foreground color/Eyedropper/Paint pot tools. Next I dragged the recolored image onto a canvas sized 15 x 15in (40 x 40cm)/2362 x 2362px/150dpi.

I duplicated the design horizontally and vertically to make a square. Now it was time to add lots of layers of detail on top of the basic design. (2)

First came the idea of the minerals that are essential to health: zinc, iron, calcium, etc. There are plenty of periodic symbols online. I cropped and recolored the background of each one to match the main image, then dragged them into place—manipulating each one to fit by using the Move tool. (3, 4)

Using my nifty digital pen, I wrote my pearls of nutritional wisdom in the spaces between the branches.

However, before I got going with the pen, I had a good look at the overall image and identified where to put the writing and symbols to get an even spread. I wrote a number in each space (which would be colored out) so that I could find the places to fill when I zoomed in close to write. (5)

Down the tree trunks I wrote a list of the foods that I include in my diet. (6)

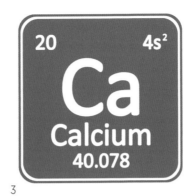

3

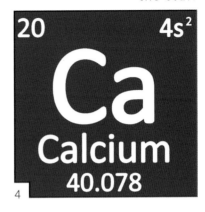

4

5

6

PROJECT drawing blood

I didn't want to color the blood vessels solid red—it's too predictable. Instead, I needed a device to convey the color and yet bring something else to the design. (7)

Aboriginal symbols describe nature and the features of the landscape—these seemed to chime very nicely with the "mother earth" theme I was exploring. (8)

Again using my digital pen, I drew little rivers of aboriginal symbols in my blood vessels. (9)

7

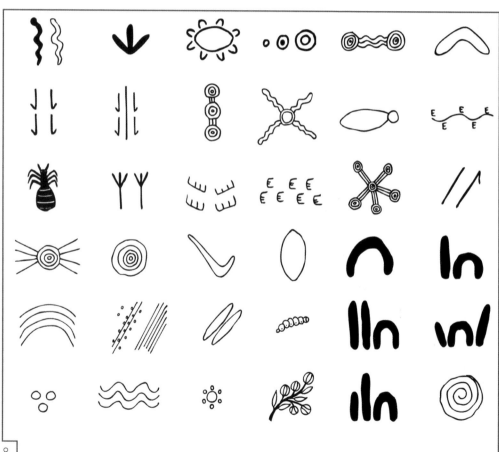

8

9

The design was coming on well but needed one more element—a soft, dynamic motif to break up the lines. I drew a big leaf (A) and a small leaf (B) then dragged them onto a single canvas for convenience. Its dimensions were 8 x 8in (20 x 20cm)/1181 x 1181px/150dpi. (10)

Using the digital pen I marked my design with yellow 1s and 2s to show where the leaves were to be dragged and dropped. I made the leaves less uniform by altering their sizes, and reversing them horizontally and vertically using the Move tool. (11)

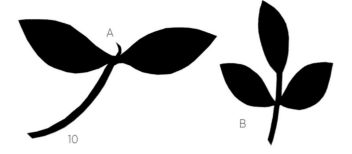

10

When I had finished adding all the elements to my design I saved the file as Artwork.jpg and made a copy.

At this point I checked that the design still worked well as a fabric when the pattern was repeated. I dragged my Artwork.jpg copy to a canvas sized 31.5 x 31.5in (80 x 80cm)/4724 x 4724px/150dpi. Then I duplicated it horizontally and vertically to fill the square. (12)

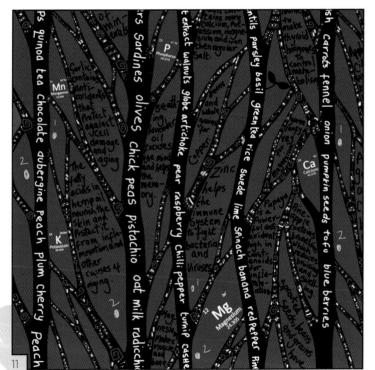

11

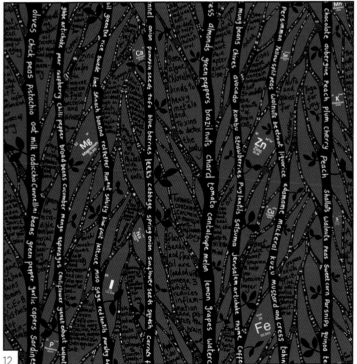

12

PROJECT drawing blood

Even though I was pleased with the way my fabric looked on the screen, it's a good idea to get a sample before going ahead and placing the order.

Here are some good reasons:
1. To check that the colors are right.
2. To see how your design looks on the fabric you have chosen—maybe it loses too much detail on linen and needs to be on crisp cotton instead?
3. Having a sample of the fabric to "offer up" on your chair will help you to decide if the design needs scaling up or down.

I cropped a 6in (15cm) strip from the top of the enlarged Artwork.jpg copy file and called it Drawing Blood Sample 1. jpg. Then I uploaded it as a sample to my online digital printers and asked that it be printed on cotton drill. (13)

What came back (top fabric) was too violet in color, and the writing wasn't very easy to read printed on cotton drill. I had acquired my chair by then and was able to see that its generous proportions needed a larger-scale print. (14)

I changed the background color on the sample to a truer blue, increased the repeat from 31.5 to 39in (80 to 100cm) and ordered a sample on Panama heavy cotton. What arrived in the post the second time around (bottom fabric) was perfect.

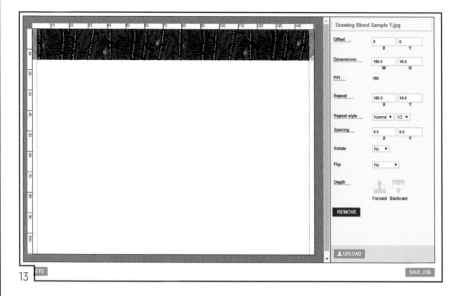

13

14

I now knew the right scale, the right color, and the right fabric. So all I had to do now was alter my original Artwork.jpg and prepare the file for printing. (15)

I dragged my original Artwork.jpg file onto a final new canvas sized 39 x 39in (100 x 100cm)—my new repeat—5906 x 5906px/150dpi. (16)

First, using Set foreground color/Color picker/Paint pot tools, I recolored the background to the new blue.

Then, using the Offset tool, I tided up the joins that would come together when the fabric was repeated, both horizontally and vertically.

I saved the file as Drawing Blood Fabric.jpg. It was ready to upload to the online digital fabric printers.

I measured-up the chair and estimated that I needed 11ft 6in (3.50m)—which turned out to be exactly right. (*See* the fabric/quantifying.)

After I received the second sample I chose to print my design on heavy Panama cotton, which is an excellent fabric for a busy design like this. All the detail that I had painstakingly put in would come back loud and clear. Panama is also a hard-wearing (310gsm/9oz per sq yd), informal fabric that suited the style and mood of the project.

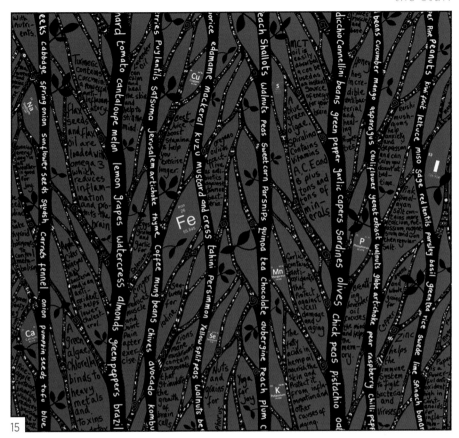

15

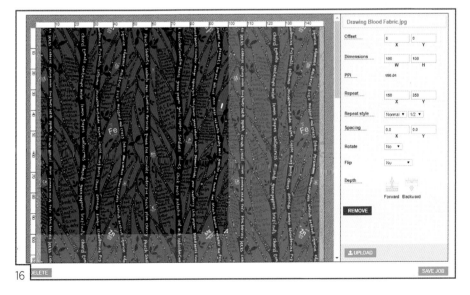

16

17

The Chair

Once I had settled on the idea of a linear design of tree trunks and blood vessels, I was on the look-out for a big curvy armchair to show off the lines. I found this fellow very cheap on eBay. It was a bit unloved, very lumpy, and the cushion was missing, but I thought it had loads of potential for reworking into a more generous shape. (17)

My plan was to accentuate the roundness of the arms and really build them up so they looked almost circular from the side. I planned to change the platform seat into an equally overblown, over-stuffed seat. Finally, I hoped to remodel the inside back so that I could do away with the buttons and make it a cleaner design.

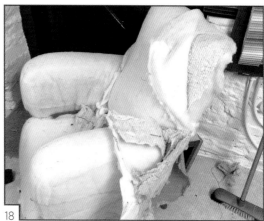

18

19

At first glance the chair looked in pretty good condition, but I could tell that it largely consisted of lumpy old wool felt and polyester which had to go—but not go to waste! I saved all the wool felt for stuffing the cavities of the outside back and arms, and kept the old polyester to shred and stuff into cushion pads. (18)

Underneath the upholstery I discovered the frame was part metal with a decent spring unit in the seat. The sprung back was in good condition with a layer of rubberized hair that I decided to leave in place. (19)

Arms

I made a tarpaulin (or heavy hessian) cover for each arm to block in the inside and outside arm and make a platform for the new foam. As I was working on a metal frame, I had to make a template and sew the pieces together. On a wooden frame I would have just stapled the tarp in place. (20)

I made the shape of the arms by building up thin layers of foam. The first layer was a 1.9in (5cm) piece of very firm 6lb (2.7kg) chip foam, glued in place with spray adhesive and shaped using a shape knife. (21, 22)

This was followed by lots of layers of 0.6in (1.5cm) blue (firm seating) foam; each layer attached with spray adhesive and shaped in the same way with a knife. I had to draw on my sculpting skills for this job. (23)

I sat on the arms in between layers to ensure that the construction was solid and that the adhesive had stuck. (24)

Next I glued a layer of 1in (2.5cm) foam to the outside arm and the inside arm, drawing around the arc of the new sculpted foam to get the shape right. Using the two cut pieces of foam from the first arm as a template for the second arm helped to keep the arms symmetrical. (25, 26)

I glued the edges of the foam together and glued a strip of polyester over each seam to hold them firmly in place.

25

26

27

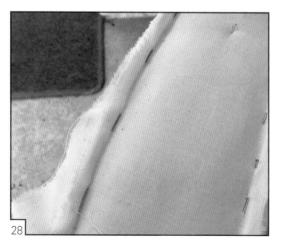

28

Template

I made a template of the new round shape in calico (only on one arm). This template would be used to make a fixed calico cover for each arm, as well as a pattern to cut the top fabric. (27)

I cut a panel of calico that ran the length of the top of the arm (plus a bit extra at both ends). This panel was 1.2in (3cm) wider than the width of the last foam panel underneath—giving a 0.6in (1.5cm) seam allowance either side.

I cut two pieces of calico big enough to cover the inside arm and the outside arm, plus enough for generous tuck-ins and turnings.

A few anchor pins held the calico pieces in place where I wanted them on the foam. Then I pinned together the two long circular seams that ran the length of the arm. I was very careful to keep the panel on the top of the arm straight, and took my time getting the template absolutely perfect. It's well worth all this effort when you eventually slide the top cover onto the chair and it fits like a well-made suit. (28)

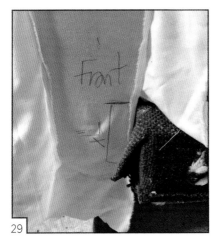

29

Before I took the template off the chair I drew clear notes on the calico (with a ballpoint pen, my marker of choice) to show which piece is which—inside arm/outside arm/arm panel—plus any notes to leave a bit of extra fabric where necessary. I also drew an arrow on each piece of calico pointing to the top of the chair, at right angles to the floor. This helped to keep the pattern straight when I cut out the top fabric. (29)

30

I like to make all the cuts that are necessary to the calico template, and copy them onto the top cover; that way there's no risk of making a mistake with the expensive top fabric. (30)

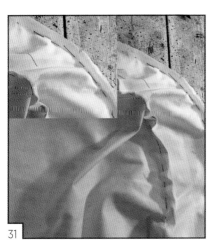

31

I carefully lifted the calico template off the arm, leaving just the pins in the two long seams. Then I trimmed the seams to 0.6in (1.5cm) and randomly snipped in a few little notches, so that the pattern pieces could be reassembled in exactly the right place. (31)

Out came all the pins and I ironed the lovely pattern pieces; inside arm, outside arm, arm panel. I cut two copies of each pattern piece.

After matching notches and pinning, I machine-sewed the pieces together to make two calico arm covers. I temporary-tacked them onto the arms. The original calico template will be used to cut the top fabric. (32)

32

33

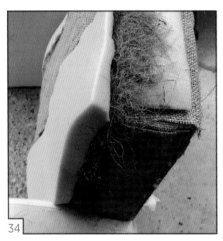

34

35

Inside Back

The inside back was a bit soggy and in need of careful reshaping. It had a hollow rather than a swell in the lumbar region, and it fell away at the outside edges. I would have preferred a nice firm edge for my back scroll.

Again, I had to draw on my sculpting skills to get this right. First, there was a split in the rubberized hair covering the inside back, so I fixed that with a gluey hessian strip.

I stuck a 1in (2.5cm) piece of foam with a chamfered edge to the lumber region to bolster and fill out the lumber swell. (33)

Next came two wedge-shaped pieces of foam that ran either side of the inside back, then a slim panel of foam on the very top where there was a bit of a hollow. (34)

Last, I wanted to have a gentle swell along the top line of the inside back (it was still a bit sunk in the middle), so I glued a rectangular section of foam there. (35)

Over the top of these small modifications I glued a single piece of 1in (2.5cm) foam.

At this point it's important to mention the centerline on the foam, which matches up with a center mark on the top and bottom of the chair. (36)

I glued a strip of calico to the top and bottom edge of the foam and stapled it to the frame. The new scroll shape was filled in (on both sides) with two layers of foam: one piece of 0.6in (1.5cm) cut to fit the scroll (I drew around the scroll itself to get the shape), and one slightly smaller 1in (2.5cm) piece to pad it out underneath. (37)

Both layers of the scroll were glued in place, then the edges of the top scroll and the inside back were glued together (the same as the outside and inside arm), and polyester strips were glued over the joins.

36

37

Now I was ready to make the template for the inside back.

I cut a piece of calico wide enough—and long enough—to cover the inside back, allowing generous tuck-ins and turnings. I folded it exactly in half and cut a tiny notch in the center, top, and bottom. Then I drew a vertical line in ballpoint pen from notch to notch. I laid this line directly on top of the line that ran down the center of the inside-back foam. Then I put some anchor pins around the line to keep it all in place.

Then I cut another piece of calico big enough to comfortably cover the area of the scroll, and anchor-pinned that in place too. I clearly marked each calico piece—inside back/back scroll—and drew arrows pointing to the top of the chair, at right angles to the floor.

Then I carefully pinned the scroll seam together, checking from time to time how it looked from the front. It's easy to get a crooked seam if you look at it only from the side.

Note: I know you're probably thinking that the scroll is not pinned on the edge, but much farther back. Trust me—look at the image (bottom right) . . . . am I right? (38)

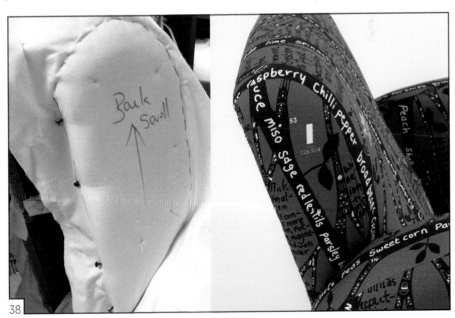

38

PROJECT drawing blood

I lifted the template off the inside back leaving only the scroll seam pins. Then I trimmed the seam to 0.6in (1.5cm) and snipped random notches, the same way as before for the arm template.

I unpinned the template seam, laid the inside-back piece on a table, and folded it in half down the centerline. A few pins stopped it moving about while I cut around the template shape, making a mirror image—not forgetting to cut the notches. When I took the pins out and opened it up, I had a beautiful, symmetrical inside-back pattern piece.

I used the template to cut one more calico inside back, and two more calico back scrolls. Now I had two scrolls and an inside back to machine-sew together, plus a scroll and an inside back to use as a pattern to cut the top fabric.

I temporary-tacked, and then stapled, the calico cover onto the inside back. (39)

Seat

I used four layers of 1in (2.5cm) foam to start building up the seat and thoroughly spray-glued each layer as I added them. (40)

I could have used a single piece of 3.9in (10cm) foam or eight bits of 0.6in (1.5cm) foam; I just happened to have a lot of 0.6in cutoffs to use up. It's actually not a bad idea to use lots of layers to remodel a seat because you can try out the height after each layer. Note the centerline on each piece of foam.

A single piece of 1in foam went over the top of the layers— cut long enough to cover the front panel of the seat. I glued calico strips to the back and side edges of this piece of foam and stapled them to the frame. (41)

I glued a chamfered-edge rectangle of 1in foam under the final layer of seat foam to give the front panel of the seat a "tummy." Then I glued a strip of calico to the bottom edge of the seat foam and stapled under the front of the seat. (42)

43

The little seat scrolls were made in the same way as the back scrolls. Each scroll has two layers of foam: one 0.6in (1.5cm) piece the same shape as the scroll, and a 1in (2.5cm) piece cut slightly smaller to go under it and pad it out. I glued both the scroll shapes in place, then glued the edges of the top scroll to the seat foam, and finally glued a strip of polyester over the joins. (43)

I made a calico template of the seat in the same way as the inside back. When you do this, remember to carefully lay the calico centerline together with the foam centerline. Take your time and keep checking that the scroll looks straight from the front as well as from the side. Don't forget to write on both pieces—seat and seat scroll—and remember the arrows and notches! (44)

The remodeling, template, and calico stage were now complete.

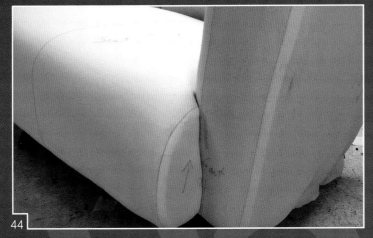

44

Note: Before I moved on I took a moment to assess how pleasing the shape of my chair was in its new calico cover.

I tried out the seat. Was it comfortable? Did I need to alter anything?

I thought the lumber swell on the inside back was still lacking bulk. I fixed this by gluing a chamfered rectangle of 0.6in (1.5cm) foam to the area (straight onto the calico) and blending it in by gluing three layers of polyester over the top. (45)

Job done—time to move on.

45

Cutting Out

This is the best bit.

I had three beautiful calico templates ready to go: arm, inside back, and seat. Time to spread my fabulous fabric out on the table and decide how best to place the design on the chair.

The drawing blood fabric tells a linear story. So my main objective with the cutting was to ensure that all the writing and mineral symbols featured at least once on the chair.

I used the same black and white tree motif across the tops of both arms. This, as it turned out, was the only exact match on the chair.

For the rest of the pieces I followed the line of the black and white tree motif, but didn't try to exactly match the pattern.

These are the areas I had to roughly pattern match: inside back to the seat, inside back to the outside back, outside arm to inside arm. (46)

The four scroll-pattern pieces I placed randomly on the fabric to make sure I included all of the mineral symbols. (47, 48)

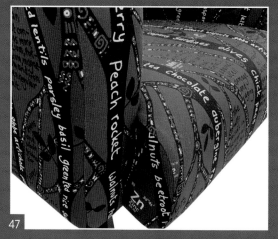

Top Cover

When I had cut out all the pattern pieces I reassembled them with pins, matched all the notches, and machine-sewed them together.

I slid each beautifully fitting piece of sewing in place and temporary-tacked them to the frame. Before I tacked down the outside arm, I grabbed all the old wool felt that had come off the chair when I stripped it down, and carefully laid it in the cavity of the outside arm. This provided a bit of extra support for the inside arm and made the new disk-shaped arms feel really solid. (49)

Then I stapled all the fabric to the frame.

The outside back was blocked in with calico (use any other piece of stout cloth you have spare). Then the outside-back fabric was pinned in place and attached with black-headed gimp pins. (50)

To finish, I tacked a new black base cloth to the bottom of the chair and celebrated with a cup of camomile tea and a few star jumps.

49

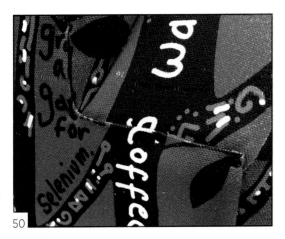

50

Roughly pattern matched: inside back to outside back

Roughly pattern matched: inside arm to outside arm

the stuff

I love my phone, don't you?

I love a beer and a bit of cake by the TV.

I love running and podcasts and seaweed
and bedtime.

I love apples and cats and money and yoga and home
and good books and friends and carrots.

I love eggs and work and chillies and hammers . . .

I think you've probably got it by now.

1

The theme of the exhibition was "Domestic Bliss." I'd been asked to make a piece of furniture to sit alongside the artists' work at the bowie gallery in my home town of Totnes in Devon, southwest England.

I lay on my mat in yoga that evening with my mind blank—not in a good way—trying to think of an idea.

Thoughts drifted in and out . . . I love yoga . . . aubergine for supper . . . I love aubergine . . . (1)

Bingo.

I made a list of all the stuff that I love.

The Chair

I'd recently downsized my workshop and found this little chair forgotten and alone at the back of my store—its time had come!

It had dark cherry-stained woodwork and a classic 1980s cut-velvet cover, but the shape was clean and simple, and it had great bolt-on legs and arms. I liked the idea of putting a circular motif down one side of a chair instead of bang in the middle as usual—and its simple shape was perfect for that treatment.

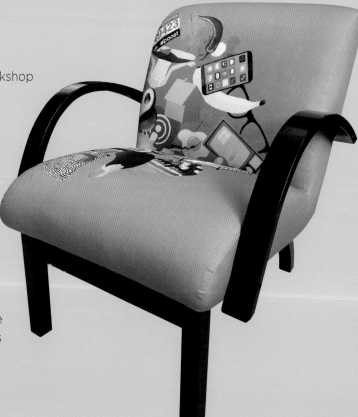

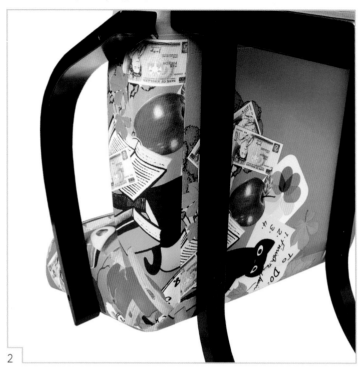

2

3

I only encountered one problem with the frame. When I unbolted the legs and arms, instead of popping the bolts into a clearly marked envelope and stowing them somewhere safe, I lost them. Finding replacements was a great deal harder than you might think: in fact it was a nightmare. Let's all learn something from that.

I gave the unbolted legs and arms my usual black paint and polish treatment. (*See* the frame/finishing.)

Unusually for a modern mass-produced chair, I discovered that it had a metal frame and just one wooden rail at the back of the seat. Tricky.

The foam upholstery was in good shape and in need of only a couple of fresh layers of polyester. Because of the metal construction of the frame, the top cover had to be made in one piece like a well-fitting slip cover (including the base)—meaning that I would have to hand-sew the cover onto the chair at the base. (2)

First, I made a calico template that covered the whole of one side of the chair, including the base. (For template making, see *lovely ovaries* and *drawing blood*.) Before I removed the pinned template from the chair I drew a circle on the calico where I wanted the stuff motif to be on the chair. I made the center of the circle at the point where the seat meets the inside back (where I placed the sun on the design). (3)

From this center point I measured and marked 17.7in (45cm) (this is approximately two thirds of the width of the seat) all the way around until I had a 35.5in (90cm) circle drawn on the calico template (including on the base). I now had a guide on my calico pattern pieces for getting the circular motif in the right place on the chair.

PROJECT the stuff
The Fabric

Photoshop

I found a circle online, cropped it and dragged it onto a new canvas sized 39 x 39in (100 x 100cm/5906 x 5906px/150dpi. I called the file Artwork.

The sky in David Hockney's painting *Bigger Splash* was the pure blue I had in mind for this design. Using the Set foreground color and Eyedropper tools I sampled the color from a downloaded image of the painting, then colored the circle with the Paint pot tool. Only the circle needed to be colored at this stage: it would serve as a guide while I assembled all the objects in a perfect sphere. (4)

4

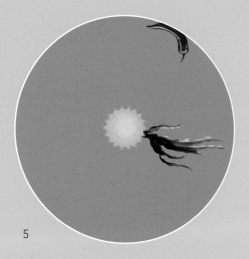
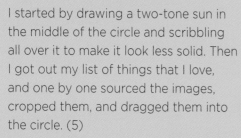

5

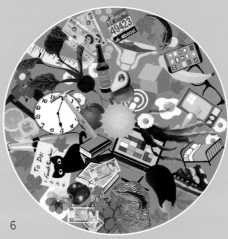

6

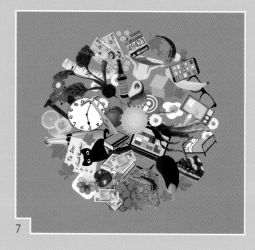

7

I started by drawing a two-tone sun in the middle of the circle and scribbling all over it to make it look less solid. Then I got out my list of things that I love, and one by one sourced the images, cropped them, and dragged them into the circle. (5)

I have to say it took ages—but I was really pleased with the result. (6)

Once I had crammed all this stuff into the circle, I colored the rest of the background blue using the Paint pot tool. (7)

I knew from my calico template that the circular motif had to be 35.5in (90cm) wide and that I needed 11.8in (30cm) of plain blue fabric either side of the motif to reach the seam on the other side of the seat. That gave me a horizontal measurement of 59in (150cm). Vertically, I needed only approximately 5.9in (15cm) on either end of the motif: I rounded the measurement up to a total of 49in (125cm). I dragged the file Artwork onto a new canvas sized 59 x 49in (150 x 125cm)/8858 x 7382px/150dpi. I centered the motif (making sure it measured 35.5in/90cm across) and used the Paint pot tool to paint the extended background to match the brilliant Californian blue sky. I saved the file as Stuff Fabric.jpg and uploaded it to the online fabric printers. (8, 9)

8

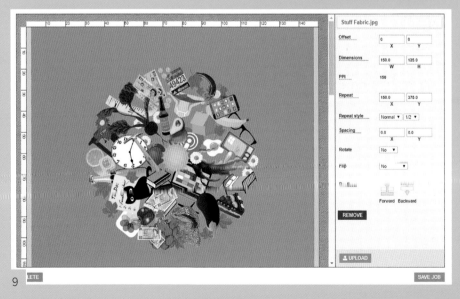

9

PROJECT the stuff

I had chosen to print my design on my go-to fabric for designs with lots of detail; namely 59in (150cm) wide Panama heavy cotton. It was difficult to quantify the amount of fabric I'd need. In theory the design could match in six places. I estimated that three repeats of the pattern would give me plenty to play with: that came to a little over 12ft (3.75m).

I had a tight deadline on this job, so there was no time to get a sample of my design. Luckily all was well when it came back from the printers, but it's a good idea if you have the time and the budget. (10)

10

Top Cover

I laid the calico pattern pieces on the fabric, matching the drawn circle to the printed motif.

In reality there were four places on the chair where the pattern could match exactly: inside back to back scroll, seat to seat scroll, inside back to seat, outside back to base. The remaining two seams—outside back to back scrol, seat scroll to base—just had to follow the circular shape but not pattern match. (11, 12, 13)

11

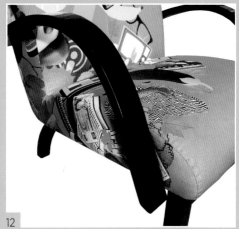
12

13

50

Once all the pieces were cut, pinned, and machine-sewn together, I had a final element to add to the slip cover. There was only one wooden rail on the metal chair frame (at the back of the seat) and I planned to make good use of it. I machine-sewed a panel of calico to the seam allowance where the inside back was joined to the seat. When the cover was complete and in place on the chair (before I hand-sewed the base) I pulled the calico panel tight (through the gap between the inside back and the seat) and stapled it to the wooden rail. (14)

14

Once the cover was really tight on the chair, I pinned and hand-sewed the base in place and finished by bolting the legs and arms back on the frame. Finally, I placed my yoga teacher on the chair and expressed my gratitude for the stuff that I love. (15)

15

catfish

Two of my fascinations collide on this fabric: Japanese art

and black and white catfish eels.

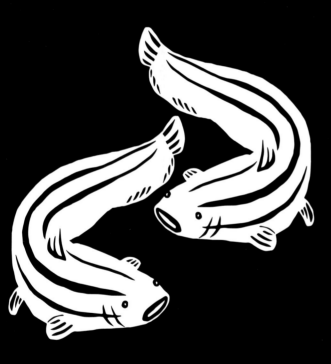

The Chair

As is so often the case I intercepted this snazzy little armchair en route to its final destination—the local garbage dump. Luckily most people who know me wouldn't dream of throwing out a chair without driving by my workshop first. They invariably leave with an empty car and a look of incredulity.

Parker Knoll fireside chairs like these were mass-produced from the 1950s onward, so they're a common sight in thrift stores, second-hand listings, and skips. Grab them!

They're comfortable, well-made chairs that reupholster handsomely. I've included four Parker Knoll projects in this book: *test card*, *microbia*, *double helix*, and this beauty, *catfish*. The method of upholstery is much the same for all of them and is explained fully in this project. (1)

1

PROJECT catfish

The Fabric

Catfish is a good example of how to design a fabric to fit the shape and size of a chair. The scale of the *catfish* fabric design was based on the widest measurement across the top of the inside back.

Print by Papa Osmubal

Linocut by Christine Bernards

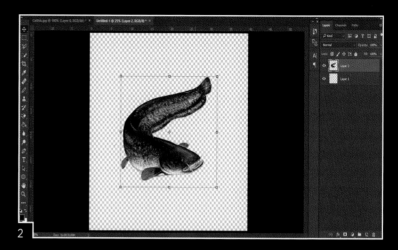

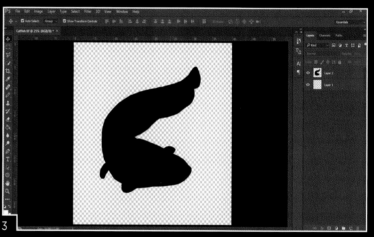

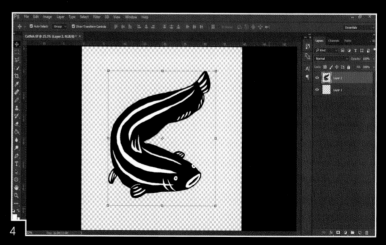

Photoshop

I started my design by searching the Internet for photos of writhing catfish eels. I found four lovely bendy examples and downloaded them to a separate file on my laptop. I uploaded the first eel to Photoshop and used the Magic eraser tool to get rid of the background. I made a new canvas sized 16 x 16in (40 x 40cm)/2362 x 2362px/150dpi. This is the actual width and drop of the *catfish* design as it will appear on the printed fabric. (2)

I dragged the eel onto the canvas and used the Set foreground color/Color picker/Paint pot tools to paint it black so that I had a blank canvas to work on (whiskers came later). (3)

This is always the tricky bit for me—drawing. I wanted the eels to look like a cross between a black and white linocut and a traditional Japanese carp (opposite).

Using the digital pen I carefully drew the white lines that would   I hoped—create the effect of a linocut. As a species they look like a combination of eel, carp, and catfish—a sort of hybrid. Even though my artwork was quite crude I hoped it would be good enough in a tumble of other black and white fish. (4)

I saved each fish as I went along as Eel 1.tif and 2, 3, and 4. When all the fish were lined up ready to go, I made a new canvas sized 16 x 16in (40 x 40cm)/2362 x 2362px/150dpi.

Remember, this was the actual size that the catfish design would be on the finished fabric with a 16in (40cm) horizontal repeat and 16in (40cm) vertical repeat.

One by one I dragged and dropped the fish onto the new canvas and set about positioning them in a pattern of organized chaos. I duplicated the eel images and flipped them horizontally to add more variety to the shapes. Finally, using the digital pen, I drew a set of whiskers on each catfish. When I was happy with the overall look, I used the Offset tool to make the repeat work vertically (the fish weren't going to repeat horizontally). (5)

For the background color I found an image of red Japanese folding paper online and downloaded it. Using the Set foreground color and Eyedropper tools, I sampled the color from the downloaded image and changed the background color to red using the Paint pot tool. I saved the image as Catfish.jpg. (6)

5

6

7

I wanted to add a motif that would bring more of a Japanese look to the design, so I made a new canvas sized 2.4 x 16in (6 x 40cm)/354 x 2362px/150dpi. Again, I was sticking to the actual size of the finished design. With the addition of a 2.4in (6cm) panel either side of the fish motif my design would be 20.5in (52cm) wide: the measurement of the widest part of the inside back on the chair. On this I used a digital pen to draw a simple linear design of wobbly black lines against a white background. (7)

I made a new canvas sized 7.8 x 16in (20 x 40cm)/1181 x 2362px/150dpi. Then dragged the black and white design into the middle of the new canvas and, using the digital pen, drew some stitches and tassels in the same red as the background. Then used a thin black line to add some detail to the red. I saved this image as Catfish Edge.tif. (8)

8

Now all that was needed was to bring the two elements together. I had already decided to print the design on hopsack cotton, a quite heavy, textured fabric, 57in (145cm) wide. I thought the detail of the design would print well enough on a textured fabric and benefit from looking a bit grainy. I made a new canvas sized 57 x 16in

(145 x 40cm)/8563 x 2362px/150dpi. Then I dragged the Catfish.jpg and Catfish Edge.tif onto the new canvas. I duplicated each motif until I had filled the width. Finally, I flattened the layers and saved the file as Catfish Fabric.jpg. The design was ready to print. (9)

9

I uploaded my design to the online fabric printers and ordered 9.8ft (3m) of hopsack. (*See* the fabric/quantifying.) (10)

The Chair

I had black and white catfish eels swimming around in my imagination for quite a while, so it was a relief when they slid out of my head and onto a fabric design. Now I could concentrate on my classic Parker Knoll armchair with the rare and exciting addition of inset armrests—premium!

I started by stripping off the old top cover, which I put in the textile recycle bin at the local dump. The upholstery on a fireside chair is very simple: a tension-sprung seat, a wool-felt pad on the inside back, and a box cushion. The fabric covering on the tension springs was a bit frayed but that didn't matter too much since I was planning to cover them. All that mattered was the anchoring strip that the springs were attached to, and that was pretty solid. The inside back was in good shape, too, and needed minimal attention. My kind of project.

I wiped the frame clean with mild soapy water and assessed the wood. These old Parker Knolls were never made from beautiful show wood: that's why they were usually heavily stained and varnished in a factory spray booth. I invariably give them my black paint treatment. I think it's fair to say that this particular chair looked ridiculously good with a black frame. (*See* the frame/finishing.) (11, 12, 13)

Once the frame was painted and polished I carefully bound the legs in calico scraps to protect them from getting bashed in the workshop.

Inside Back

First, I found the center of the frame on the outside back and made clear marks, top and bottom. These would be my guide for all the layers to come. All I had to do to the inside back was glue a couple of layers of polyester on top of the original wool-felt covering, using plenty of spray adhesive. I trimmed it neatly around the edge of the inside back to keep it sharp. (14, 15)

Then I had the pleasure of rolling out the *catfish* hopsack fabric, which I might add had turned out even more striking than I imagined. This is the first fabric I have had printed on a pigment printer; a cheaper, greener option. I was very pleased with the results. (*See* the fabric/printing.) I would usually spend a bit of time working out how best to place the pattern on the chair, but this design was tailor-made to fit. (16)

I measured and cut out the fabric for the inside back: I folded it in half lengthways and cut a tiny notch in the center, top, and bottom. Matching the notches to the center marks on the frame, I temporary-tacked the fabric to the inside back, at first by pulling it very tightly from the top to the bottom—not from side to side. It turned out that the angels of upholstery were looking down on me that day—my chair had screw-in arms! That meant that all I had to do was take out the screw holding the arm in place on either side of the chair, and slide the fabric past the arms before screwing them back in again. Had the angels been looking the other way I would have had to make a couple of tricky, downward sloping "V" cuts in the fabric before I could bring it around the arms and tack it to the outside back. (17)

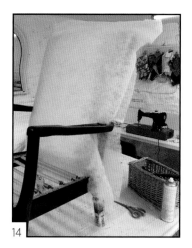
14

15

16

Screw-in arm
17

I finished the top of the inside back with a simple fold on each corner. The bottom of the inside back was turned under and attached to the frame with black-headed gimp pins. (18)

I made a corner cut either side to bring the bottom of the fabric around to the outside back. (19)

The fabric in between the corner cut and the bottom edge of the inside back was folded under diagonally and attached to the frame with black-headed gimp pins. All Parker Knoll fireside chairs have this slightly messy arrangement at the bottom of the inside back; though you can't really see the bottom of the inside back when the seat is finished. I think it's important to make it look presentable.

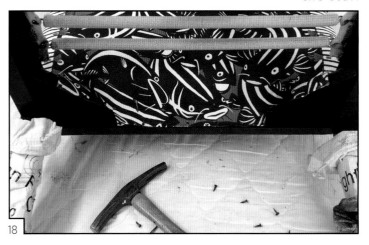

18

19

Outside Back

First, I stapled a piece of calico over the outside back cavity to make a firm base for the top fabric. You could use any similar spare fabric for this job, it's a good way to use up remnants.

Then I measured and cut out the outside back fabric, following the linear design from the inside back. Again, I folded it lengthways and cut a tiny center notch top and bottom.

I matched the notches to the center marks on the chair, the fabric was first turned under and pinned in place then attached with black-headed gimp pins. (20, 21)

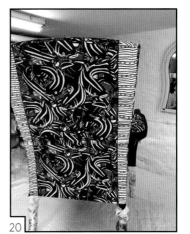

20

21

22

23

24

Armrests

As I mentioned before, this fireside chair had a pair of the classiest armrests I'd ever seen.

I simply unscrewed them from the frame and stripped them back down to the wood.

Using the wood as a template, I cut out two pieces of 0.6in (1.5cm) blue foam and chamfered the edges with a pair of scissors to soften the shape. I glued the foam to the wood with spray adhesive and glued a layer of polyester over the foam. (22, 23)

I cut two pieces of fabric approximately 1in (2.5cm) bigger than the wood. First, I temporary-tacked the fabric in place. Next I stapled the fabric tightly to the underside of the wood. Finally, I trimmed off the excess fabric and screwed the armrests back on the frame. (24)

Seat

Now it was time to transform the scruffy-looking tension-sprung seat. The springs were exposed on the original design and just the front edge (from the third spring) was upholstered. I was planning to make a piece of sewing that would encase the springs in a black cloth cover (top and bottom), with a panel of the top fabric machine-sewn to the black cloth at the front edge. This is not a complicated process, but it's just a bit tricky to put into words. I hope the photos will help—here goes!

I started by cutting a piece of black cloth long enough to cover the seat and the front edge twice (double), and wide enough to cover the front edge, plus 0.8in (2cm) turnings on either side. To keep everything straight, I made a centerline down the long piece of black cloth with a few pins, then I marked the center of the inside back (on the chair) with a pin. Finally, I marked the center of the front edge of the frame with a ballpoint pen. I passed the black cloth around the spring nearest the inside back and under all the seat springs to the front edge. Now the springs were encased.

The seat tapered toward the back of the chair, so I tucked in the sides of the black cloth (top and bottom) to fit. The side edges would ultimately be nailed down to the frame with gimp pins, so there was no necessity to machine-finish them.

I cut a piece of the top fabric to generously cover the width of the front edge horizontally, and vertically deep enough to cover the first three springs and the front edge, plus turnings.

I machine-sewed a neatening double hem at the bottom of the fabric piece and marked the centers with a pin on the top and bottom.

There were two lines of machine-sewing in my spring/front edge cover. The first was at the back of the cover (next to the last spring). The second line of sewing attached the fabric panel to the black cloth (where it met the third spring from the front).

For the first machine-sewn line I made sure that the black cloth was touching the inside back, and put a line of pins up against the spring nearest the inside back (through both layers of black cloth). For the second line to be machine-sewn I pinned the top fabric across the front edge to the

black cloth where it met the third spring (only through the top layer of the black cloth).

Once the two lines were pinned in place, I carefully lifted the black cloth with the attached fabric from the seat. Then I machine-sewed the two lines where I had pinned them, at the back of the seat and attaching the top fabric panel to the black cloth. Now the sewing was complete and ready to fit on the seat. First, I wrapped the black cloth around the spring nearest the inside back and brought the bottom layer all the way to the front edge.

The top layer of the black cloth was tucked under the third spring at the front and the (attached) top fabric panel went over the top of the third spring at the front. (25)

I stapled both layers of the black cloth at either side of the front edge. Using a curved needle and stout thread, I hand-stitched the two layers of black cloth together (encasing the first spring) at the front edge. (26)

At this point I pushed a piece of polyester under the third front spring, deep enough to make two neat layers to cover the front edge. (27)

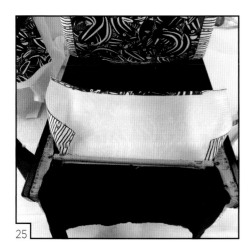

Hand-sawn edge

25

26

27

28

29

30

31

Finally, I pulled the top fabric panel over the polyester and tucked it under the outside edges. I attached the back corners of the black cloth and outside edges of the fabric front panel to the frame with black gimp pins. (28–31)

. . . and relax.

The Cushion

A seat cushion is an opportunity to think outside the box—if you'll pardon the pun. All the Parker Knoll projects in the book have slight variations on a standard box cushion, with the exception of *test card* which has an extra-tall box cushion (to display a Buddhist chant). (32–34)

32

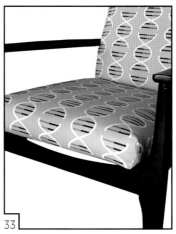

33

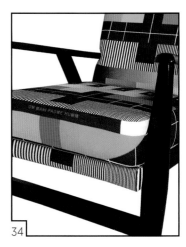

34

The original cushion on this chair was missing, but I would guess that the foam had perished and certainly wouldn't comply with modern safety standards. When it comes to seat cushions I find it's best to start from scratch and make my own. I always keep a roll of 0.6in (1.5cm) blue (firm seating) foam in stock, so whenever I'm ready to tackle a cushion of whatever shape or size, I can just get on with it. The 0.6in (1.5cm) foam is easy to layer-up and sculpt into any shape.

On the *catfish* frame there was a definite point to the front edge that I planned to echo in the shape of the cushion. I started by measuring the depth and (tapering) width measurements of the seat. In order to get a pointy front edge on the cushion, I cut four layers of 0.6in (1.5cm foam)—according to my measurements—making each layer approximately 0.4in (1cm) longer at the front edge. Then I drew a clear centerline on each piece of cut foam. Each layer was glued together (keeping the center lines matching) using plenty of spray adhesive on both surfaces. (35)

35

Layers 5 and 6 were glued in place (top and bottom) and joined together along the top of the front edge, covering all the staggered foam edges at the front. (36)

36

Using a large carving knife, I chopped the corners off the back edge of the cushion to match the curve of the inside back on the chair. (37)

37

Then I wrapped and glued a single layer of polyester around the top and bottom of the foam and glued a piece of polyester on each side panel. I glued the seams together following the lines of the box cushion, trimming the seams when they were dry. Now the cushion was neatly encased in polyester. (38)

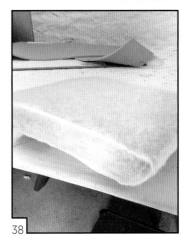

38

I drew a clear line around the center, front, and back. (39)

39

Next up, the calico cushion template, which served two purposes. First, I used it as a pattern to cut the top fabric. Second, once the fabric is cut, the calico pattern pieces are sewn together to make a cover for the foam and polyester cushion. I started by cutting a rectangle of calico long enough to cover the top and bottom of the cushion in one piece.

I cut another piece for the cushion zipper panel at the back, and last, a piece for the cushion side panel (only one).

I folded the main calico piece lengthways and cut a tiny notch top and bottom. Then I drew a line from notch to notch in ballpoint pen. I laid the calico line on top of the line that ran around the cushion and held it in place with a few anchoring pins. I then pinned the zipper panel and cushion side panel in place with a few anchoring pins. Carefully following the shape of the box cushion, I pinned the seams together around the cushion side panel and around half of the zipper panel. I needed to make a template of only half of the cushion—for the other half, I could cut out a mirror image. (40)

When I had checked that all the seams were straight and that it was fitting well on the cushion, I drew an arrow pointing up on each pattern piece and wrote "top" to mark the top of the cushion. Then I took out the anchoring pins (but not the seam pins!) and took the calico template off the cushion. Next I trimmed the seams to 0.6in (1.5cm) and cut a few random notches along the seams which will later help to match the pattern pieces back together again. (41)

I took out the seam pins and laid the main, central calico pattern piece on the table and folded it down the centerline from notch to notch. I put in a few pins to hold it steady then cut out the pattern, copying the shape to the other side of the cushion cover. I did the same with the zipper panel: folded it down the centerline and cut out the mirror image on the other side. I cut a calico copy of the cushion side panel. Now the cushion template was complete. I had four pattern pieces: the main section (top and bottom) of the cushion, two

40

41

42

cushion side panels, and one zipper panel. I pinned all the calico pattern pieces on the *catfish* fabric (following the linear design on the cushion top and bottom) and cut them out. However, I cut the fabric zipper panel 1.2in (3cm) deeper than the template to allow for the zipper to be inserted. I drew a line across the width of the fabric panel, cut it in half, and ironed a 0.6in (1.5cm) turning along each cut edge. Then I machine-sewed in a black zipper. (42)

Once all the fabric was cut out (and the zipper panel was made) I pinned the calico template back together and machine-sewed it, leaving the back seam open for the cushion to go in. Then I hand-stitched the back seam. (43)

Now for the pointy catfish cushion cover. First pinning and matching notches, I assembled the fabric pattern pieces and machine-sewed the cushion together. I prefer to bias-bind the seams on a removable cushion cover rather than use the overlocker. In fact, I find the overlocker so problematical that I'm actually subject to a restraining order if I go too close to mine! (44)

I was intensely happy with the way this cushion turned out. (45, 46)

Just when I was establishing a fond attachment to black and white catfish eels I discovered that in India they have a giant man-eating species. I'll try not to have nightmares about that.

43

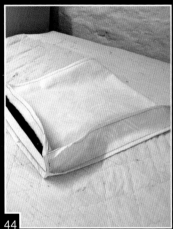

44

45

46

love me tender

It makes me smile to see how the millennials have taken the tattoo and turned it into a respectable and legitimate means of expressing who they are. It wasn't like that in 1970s Surrey; back then, a tattoo was an incendiary declaration of class and morality. Only sailors and tarts had tattoos.

I grew up in a place called Caterham Valley where there was a carnival and fun fair every summer, and from about the age of ten my friend Deb and I were allowed to go on our own.

Even at that age we knew the carnival was rubbish, but we would totter along behind the parade giggling and snickering, and generally getting over excited for the main event. The fun fair.

PROJECT love me tender

Everyone in Caterham looked like Karen or Richard Carpenter in those days, which made the boys who ran the rides at the fun fair all the more exotic and dangerous because they looked like Elvis and had tattoos. Deb and I knew that Elvis (despite being the King of Rock'n'Roll) was a bit common and looking like him was not what we did in Surrey. It was, therefore, a social certainty that looking like Elvis and being covered in tattoos was so far beyond the bounds of acceptability it was hard to conceive. And yet, we can never forget the queasy thrill of having our Waltzer chair spun harder and harder, and faster and faster, by the tattooed biceps of the boys who looked like Elvis and ran the rides. That's how an old school tattoo and a line from Elvis's *Love Me Tender* ended up on the back cushion of this little sofa—now in my sitting room. It reminds me of the beautiful bad boys who spun the Waltzer. (1)

1

The Frame

This little sofa began life as an armchair. A friend gave me a pair of rickety old (poo-splattered) chairs that had been in her outhouse for years: truth be told, I wasn't thrilled. However, I thought the arms had a pleasant jaunty angle and the idea for a simple boxy love seat began to take shape. (2, 3)

At this point I should explain that I'm not a carpenter. My woodworking skills are very basic and not very pretty, but I know how to make a furniture framework for an upholsterer and I know how to make it strong enough to do the job. So I grabbed one of the chairs and sawed off the arms. I glued

2

3

4

and screwed them to a new front and back rail, extending the seat to the length I wanted for my love seat. (4)

I made a rail for the top of the inside back and added a post to support its center. Then I added an extra layer to increase the overall height of the inside back and arms: all glued and screwed. A tacking rail was added to the bottom of the inside back, parallel to the original tacking rails on the arms. Next I glued and screwed a strengthening brace from the front rail to the back rail and glued and screwed four corner blocks to add strength and to provide a solid platform for the legs. (5)

Legs

To finish the frame I asked a local joinery company to make me a set of straight, square, screw-in legs. (6)

All I had to do was drill a hole in each corner block, hammer in the four metal tee nuts and screw in my handsome new legs. (7)

I chose to keep the legs straight to give my love seat the look of a Georgian settee. I stained the bare wood dark mahogany, then I rubbed them back with wire wool to give them a bit of a distressed look, before finishing with a dark brown wax polish. I used silver-colored aluminum embossing sheets to make a metal cap for the bottom of each leg and attached them with small dome-headed nails (3/0 x 10mm nickel on steel with normal-sized shaft but a much smaller head). (*See Kathakali.*)

First, I painted the aluminum caps with black metal paint (Hammerite) and then I distressed them with wire wool so that the nail heads shone like studs. Finally, I gave the metal caps a dark brown wax polish and nailed a dome of silence into the bottom of each leg. (8)

5

6

7

8

love me tender

The Upholstery

On this little sofa the upholstery was simplicity itself: just a series of covered pads. First of all the seat, inside back, and arms were webbed and blocked in with tarpaulin or heavy hessian.

On the seat I put 3.9in (10cm) of blue (firm seating) foam, plus a 0.6in (1.5cm) piece over the top and down the front (to soften the front edge). The inside back and arms were covered in 1.9in (5cm) foam. All the foam was glued in place with plenty of spray adhesive on both surfaces. At the edges where the foam met the frame, it was tipped under and glued, rounding off the edges. Then came the calico cover (seat, inside back, and inside arms), followed by a layer of polyester. The calico cover serves two purposes: First, it pulls the foam into shape and gets everything nice and tight ready for the top cover. Second, it gives you a practice run for the cuts and folds you will have to make to the expensive top cover. (9)

Top Cover

I chose dark gray cotton velvet by Kobe to cover the sofa and to make the back of the cushion that sits in the sofa. The top cover was mitred at the corners where the inside back meets the arm. (10)

Where the seat meets the inside arm there was a straight fold. (11)

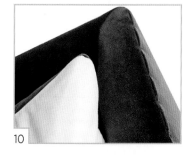

The outside arms and outside back were first blocked in with calico, before the top cover was pinned in place, then attached with tiny black-headed gimp pins. Finally, I tacked a black cotton base cloth to the bottom of the sofa. (12-14)

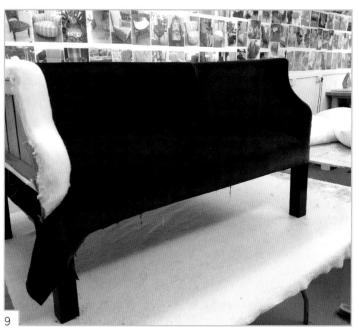

The Cushion

The inspiration for the cushion design came from the traditional tattoos that I remember from my youth, so when I found this old-school twin-heart design, I fell in love. This classic motif crops up all

over the Internet, but it's a very old image that I could find only in very low resolution, muddy images. I decided to call in a favor. (15)

I sent the original tattoo image to my son (who just happens to be a talented graphic designer). He worked his magic and returned the twin hearts in fabulous order. Essentially he started again and drew the design from scratch—which would have been way beyond

my capabilities. He also wrote "Love Me Tender" across the banners for me. All for love: what a prince! (16)

Photoshop

All I had to do was to prepare the image for printing. The finished back cushion had to measure 41 x 17.7in (105 x 45cm). The tattoo motif had to measure 16.5 x 12.5in (42 x 32cm) in the center. The printers' furnishing velvet was 51in (130cm) wide (weighing 14.6oz/416g). The file would be the width of the fabric (51in/130cm) and 19.7in (50cm) vertically to allow for turnings.

I made a new canvas sized 51 x 19.7in (130 x 50cm)/7677pc x 2953px/150dpi. First, I painted the background slightly off-white using the Set foreground color/Color picker/Paint pot tools. Then I dragged my son's beautiful artwork into the

center of the canvas and made it measure 17.7 x 11.8in (45 x 30cm). I flattened the image and saved the file as Love Me Tender Fabric.jpg. Finally I uploaded it to the online fabric printers. (17, 18)

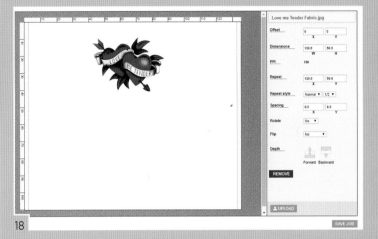

When my beautiful velvet panel arrived I made it into a long cushion to fit inside the back of the sofa (with dark gray velvet on the back and a black zipper at the bottom). The cushion interior was a made-to-measure cambric-covered feather pad. (19, 20)

Love Me Tender is my favorite Elvis song. Whenever I hear it I fall in love with him all over again . . . and I always will.

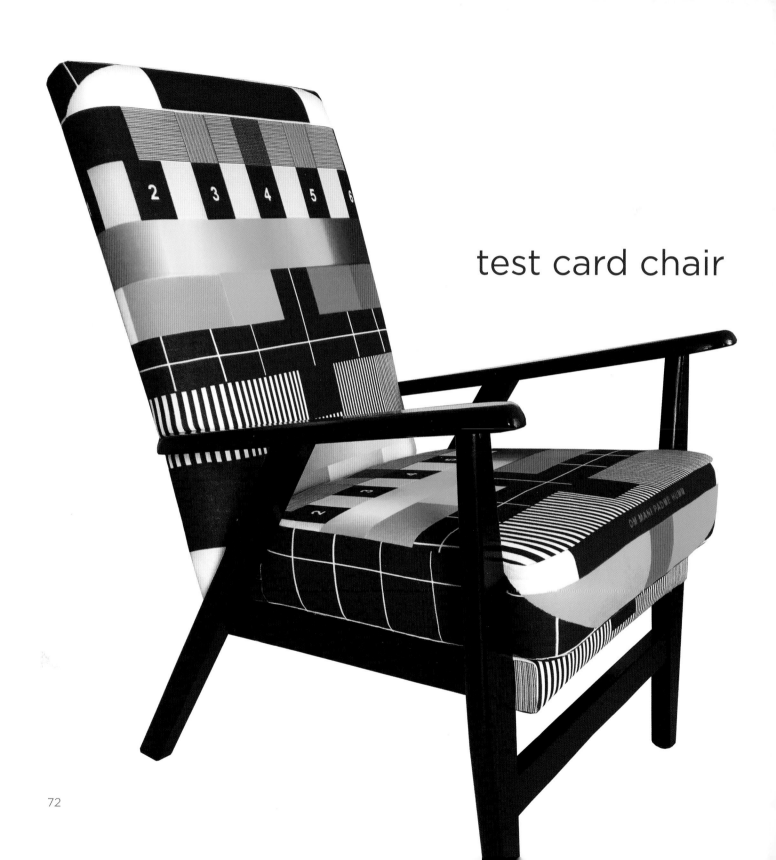

test card chair

The *test card* chair is a tribute to my dad, who was a TV repairman when I was a little girl. The image of the test card on broken TVs in my dad's workshop was part of the visual landscape of my childhood. Back then televisions with valves went wrong all the time, so I remember him being constantly on call and extremely popular—he was like one of the emergency services. Families would sit around the blank screen in stunned silence and watch him miraculously restore life to the silent black box. Before computers and iPhones, televisions were the only magic boxes we had, and my dad was a magician.

When the fabric for this chair arrived back from the printers it revealed a little secret. Along the bottom of the circular motif were some tiny blue words that I hadn't noticed. It was the Buddhist chant "Om mani padme hum." Bonus! (1)

The Fabric

There are about a million images of the BBC Test Card online, from all parts of the globe. I spotted this uncomplicated version with a simple black and white grid background and lots of vibrant color. A quick search for similar images found a further three million— isn't the Internet insane? I liked the way the dark background made the colors in the circle "pop" and the grid design worked well with my newly streamlined frame.

The Chair

This cute little fireside chair was another cheap eBay find in need of minimal modification. The upholstery, top cover, and construction of the seat and cushion are the same as the other Parker Knolls in this book (*catfish, microbia, double helix*) and fully explained in *catfish*. (2)

Once the chair was stripped down, I decided to make one small alteration to the frame. There were three shallow semicircles of wood nailed on the top of the inside back and down the sides to give the back a rounded look. Since I was planning to use a grid pattern, I thought the frame would work better if it was square, so I simply levered them off. I thought it was a pretty sound decision to paint the show wood black; it complemented the shape of the frame and looked really handsome with the *test card* fabric. (*See* the frame/finishing.) (3)

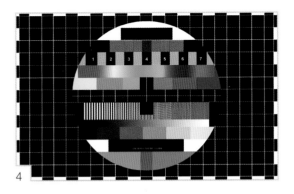

4

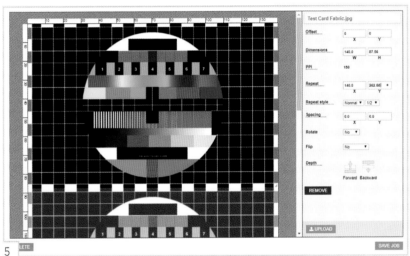

Test Card Fabric.jpg

Offset	0	0
	X	Y
Dimensions	140.0	87.56
	W	H
PPI	150	
Repeat	140.0	262.68 +
	X	Y
Repeat style	Normal ▼ 1/2 ▼	
Spacing	0.0	0.0
	X	Y
Rotate	No ▼	
Flip	No ▼	
Depth	Forward Backward	

REMOVE

↥ UPLOAD

...LETE

SAVE JOB

5

6

Photoshop

I downloaded the test card image. I had chosen to print my design on linen union that is 55in (140cm) wide—this would be the width of my artwork. The test card is rectangular, so I estimated that 39in (100cm) would be enough vertically to fit the image.

So I made a new canvas sized 55 x 39in (140 x 100cm)/8268 x 5906px/150dpi. I dragged the test card image onto the new canvas and, using the Move tool, stretched it to fit the 55in (140cm) width. Then I clicked on Maintain aspect ratio and the image adjusted back into proportion at 34.5in (87.56cm) vertically. So, using the Crop tool, I cropped the canvas to 34.5in (87.56cm). All I had to do now was flatten the image and save it as Test Card Fabric.jpg ready to upload to the online fabric printers. (4)

The vertical repeat of the pattern was 34.5in (87.56 cm), and even though it was a very small chair, I estimated that I would need three full repeats to do the job. The fabric order came to 8.5ft (2.6m). (5, 6)

Top Cover

I love the challenge of placing a large design on a tiny chair: telling the whole story on a small canvas. I wanted to center the circular motif in the middle of the inside back and make it look like it wrapped around the side of the chair to the outside back. First, I cut out the inside back, then centered the pattern on the chair, temporary-tacked, and then stapled it into place. (7)

Next I cut two outside back pieces that were a pattern match for the continuation of the circle around the chair on either side. I pinned them in place along the join between the inside and outside back. (8)

Then I pinned the two outside back pieces together down the center of the outside back.
I unpinned the sides of the outside back (keeping the center outside back pins in place) and machine-sewed and pressed the center back seam. Now the outside back with its invisible center back seam was ready to be pinned back in place where it matched the inside back. Rather than using gimp pins, I hand-sewed the outside back to the chair to keep the illusion of a continuous circle. Phew! How complicated was that to explain? (9)

The seat front (under the cushion) was covered in the black and white-striped parts of the pattern, which looked really striking next to the new black woodwork. (10)

I decided to center the Buddhist mantra on the front of the box cushion panel and center the circular motif in the middle of the cushion top. (11)

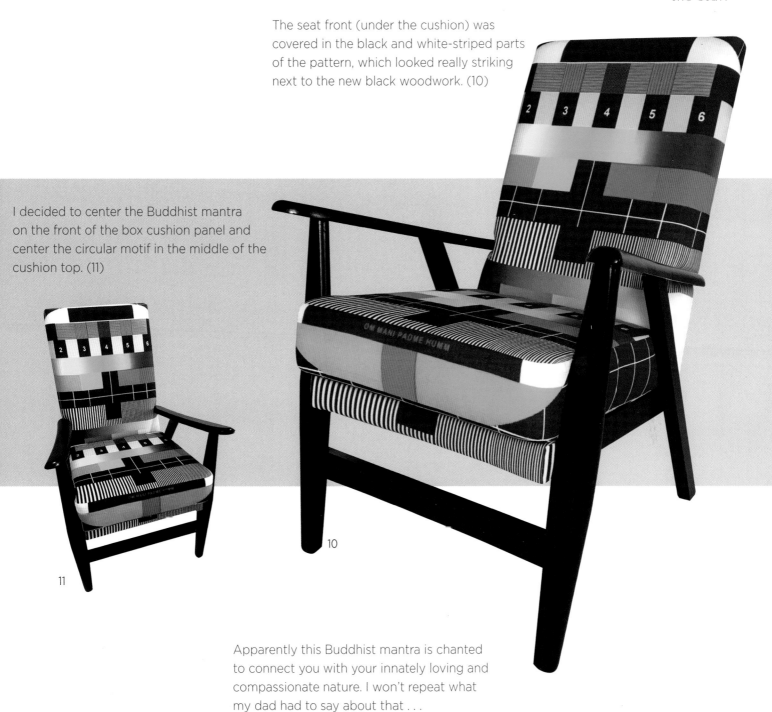

11

10

Apparently this Buddhist mantra is chanted to connect you with your innately loving and compassionate nature. I won't repeat what my dad had to say about that . . .

she's running the country

I had the idea to cover an armchair with the names of all the women in the world who had become the elected leaders of their countries: a shout-out to the girls in history who'd gotten the top job. It turns out to be quite a short list. Nowhere near enough names to cover an armchair: not quite enough to cover a crinoline or nursing chair. It does however fit quite neatly on the front sling of a deck chair if you repeat the names on the back.

Note: At the time the fabric went to the printers Theresa May was technically PM in the UK after David Cameron's resignation; however, she had yet to win an election. I also nearly included Hillary Clinton's name as she was running for president against Donald Trump . . .

SIRIMAVO BANDARANAIKE ∗ CEYLON. INDIRA GANDHI ∗ INDIA. GOLDA MEIR ∗ ISRAEL. ELISABETH DOMITIEN ∗ CENTRAL AFRICAN REPUBLIC. MARGARET THATCHER ∗ UNITED KINGDOM. MARIA DE LOURDES PINTASILGO ∗ PORTUGAL. DAME EUGENIA CHARLES ∗ DOMINICA. GRO HARLEM BRUNDHAND ∗ NORWAY. MILKA PLANINC ∗ YUGOSLAVIA. BENAZIR BHUTTO ∗ PAKISTAN. KAZIMIRA PRUNSKIENE. ∗ LITHUANIA. KHALEDA ZIA ∗ BANGLADESH. EDITH CRESSON ∗ FRANCE. HANNA SUCHOCKA ∗ POLAND. TANSU CILLER ∗ TURKEY. ADIATO DJALO NANDIGNA ∗ GUINEA BISSAU. ANNA JARA ∗ PERU. EWA KOPACZ ∗ POLAND. KIM CAMPBELL ∗ CANADA. SYLVIE KINIGI ∗ BURUNDI. AGATHE UWILINGIYIMANA ∗ SRI LANKA. RENETA INDZHOVA ∗ BULGARIA. CLAUDETTE WERLEIGH ∗ HAITI. SHEIKA HASINA ∗ BANGLADESH. JANET JAGEN ∗ GUYANA. JENNY SHIPLEY ∗ NEW ZEALAND. IRENA DEGUTIENE ∗ LITHUANIA. NYAN—OSORYN TUYAA ∗ MONGOLIA. HELEN CLARKE∗ NEW ZEALAND. MAME MADIOR BOYE ∗ SENEGAL. KHALEDA ZIA ∗ BANGLADESH. CHANG SANG ∗ SOUTH KOREA. MARIA DES NEVES ∗ SAO TOME. ANNELI JAATTEENMAKI ∗ FINLAND. BEATRIZ MERINO ∗ PERU. LUISA DIOGO ∗ MOZAMBIQUE. RADMILA SEKERINSKA ∗ MACEDONIA. YULIA TYMOSHENKO ∗ UKRAINE. CYNTHIA PRATT ∗ BAHAMAS. MARIA DO CARMO SILVEIRA ∗ SAO TOME. ANGELA MERKEL ∗ GERMANY. ANNE ENGER LAHNSTEIN ∗ NORWAY. PORTIA SIMPSON—MILLER ∗ JAMAICA. HAN MYEONGSOOK ∗ SOUTH KOREA. ZINAIDA GRECEANII ∗ MOLDOVA. MICHELE PIERRE LOUIS ∗ HAITI. SHEIKH HASINA ∗ BANGLADESH. JOHANNA SIGUROARDOTTIR ∗ ICELAND. JADRANKA KOSOR ∗ CROATIA. CECILE MANOROHANTA ∗ MADAGASCAR. KAMLA PERSAD—BISSESSAR ∗ TRINIDAD AND TOBAGO. MARI KIVINIEMI ∗ FINLAND. JULIA GILLARD ∗ AUSTRALIA ∗ IVETA RADICOVA ∗ SLOVAKIA. ROSARIO FERNANDEZ ∗ PERU. CISSE MARIAM KAIDAMA SIDIBE ∗ MALI. YINGLUCK SHINAWATRA ∗ THILAND. HELLE THORNING—SCHMIDT ∗ DENMARK. ALENKA BRATUSCK ∗ SLOVENIA. SIBEL SIBER ∗ NORTHERN CYPRUS. TATIANA TURANSKAYA ∗ TRANSNISTRIA. AMINATA TOURE ∗ SENEGAL. ERNA SOLBERG ∗ NORWAY. LAIMDOTA STRAUJUMA ∗ LATVIA. FLORENCE DUPERVAL GUILLAUME ∗ HAITI. SAARA KUUGONGELWA ∗ NAMIBIA. NATALIA GHERMAN ∗ MOLDOVA. VASSILIKI THANOU ∗ GREECE. MALIA PARNAS ∗ TRANSNISTRIA. BEATA SZYDLO ∗ POLAND.

1

The Fabric

I had a simple message to convey on this fabric, so I decided not to complicate the design; just the names and countries. I thought it would be more dynamic to run the text down the sling rather than across. The color palette I spotted somewhere in Morocco and filed away in my mind's eye to use one day—ruby and turquoise velvet against bright copper. Yum.

Photoshop

The cotton velvet I planned to use for the sling was 53in (135cm) wide. The words in my design would run across the width of the fabric. I made the vertical measurement of the sling 19.7in (50cm) (the deckchair width was 16.9in/43cm plus turnings).

I began by making a new canvas sized 53 x 19.7in (135 x 50cm)/7677 x 2953px/150dpi. I found the image of a beautiful turquoise gemstone online and downloaded it. By clicking on Set foreground color and using the Eyedropper tool to sample the color, I was able to borrow the color for the background.

Then, on a new layer using the Horizontal type tool, I typed the leaders' names and countries centrally in a deep raspberry color that I stole from an image of a raspberry. I flattened the image and saved the file as She's Running Fabric.jpg. Finally, I uploaded the file to the online digital fabric printers. The image was repeated once for the back of the sling so the order was 39in (1m) printed on cotton furnishing velvet (416 gsm). (1, 2)

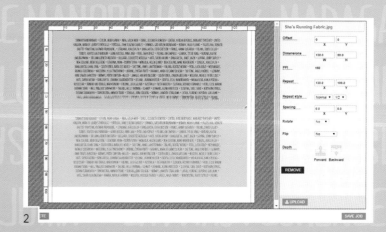

2

The Frame

Now that the fabric was on its way, I bought a new deck chair and stripped off the canvas sling (which was used to mend an old deck chair—tidy). (3)

I covered the frame with copper-colored aluminum A4 embossing sheets. These 8.3 x 11.7in (21 x 30cm) sheets are easy to find online: they feel like very thick tinfoil, are pleasing to manipulate, and can be cut with scissors. (4)

I attached the aluminum sheets with tiny domed-headed upholstery nails. 3/0 x 0.4in (10mm) nickel on steel. These have a normal sized shaft but a much smaller head. (5)

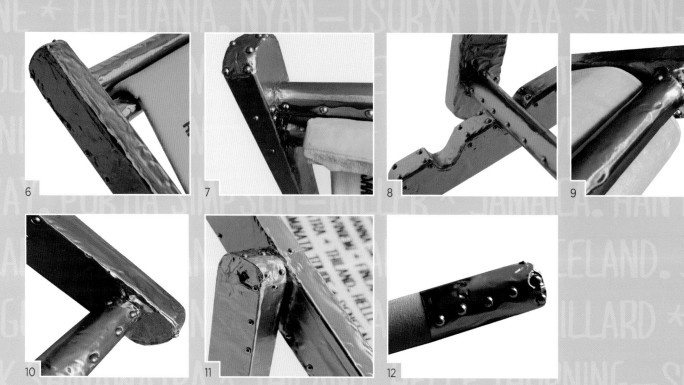

I decided that the best way to illustrate how I clad the desk chair in aluminum sheets was to include lots of photos. I promise you it's not difficult and the results are very quick and satisfying (it doesn't have to be perfect to look

impressive!). Basically, if you're good at wrapping birthday gifts, you'll be fine. Don't forget to cover the ends of the poles that hold the sling in place. (6–12)

The Upholstery

The deck chair needed a sling measuring 16.9 x 49in (43 x 124cm)—not including turnings. I cut the front and back velvet pieces to 19 x 50.7in (48 x 129cm) allowing 1in (2.50cm) turnings. The sling needed a bit of reinforcing, so I cut a piece of canvas 16.9 x 50.7in (43 x 129cm). I folded each cut piece in half lengthways to find the middle and cut a tiny notch. I started by lining up the notches and machine-sewed together (twice for strength) the three cut pieces along the top edge. The canvas piece should end up sandwiched inside the velvet sling. It goes like this: velvet wrong side, velvet right side, canvas. (13)

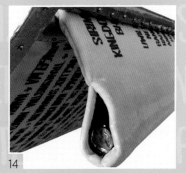

Then I tucked in the edges by 1in (2.5cm) on both sides and pinned the velvet together all the way down the length of the sling to the bottom—without forgetting to leave a gap at the top that's big enough for the pole to slide in and out comfortably. (14)

I neatly hand-sewed the two pieces of velvet together down the length of the sling on both sides. (15)

To finish the sling, I folded under the bottom edge to make a pocket big enough for the pole to slide in and out. Then I machine sewed the velvet and canvas layers together (flat, not turned under and twice for strength) and hand sewed a pretty piece of trimming over the raw edge. (16, 17)

I lit a Moroccan lantern and relaxed in my deckchair . . . whatever happened to Hillary Clinton?

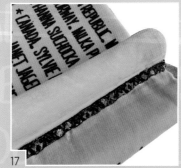

1967

The year was 1967, and Boston Marathon runner No. 261, K. Switzer, was off to a steady start.

A few minutes into the race a man ran onto the course shouting, "Get the hell out of my race and give me those numbers . . ." all the while attempting to physically pull Switzer from the track. He was Jock Stemple, the race organizer—she was Kathrine Switzer. The press photographs of the dramatic event made worldwide headlines and earned Kathrine her place in women's running history.

.

PROJECT 1967

At the time, women were barred from running competitive marathons: it would take a further five years of campaigning for Kathrine and her fellow female runners to be allowed to compete legitimately in the race. Luckily for Kathrine, her running mate in 1967 was an All-American football player and nationally ranked hammer thrower named Tom Miller.*
He had little difficulty removing Jock Stemple from the course, allowing Kathrine to continue with the race. She said "I knew if I quit, nobody would ever believe that women had the capability to run 26 miles." She did it in four hours two minutes.

I salute Kathrine Switzer.

Once I had settled on the idea of a tribute to Kathrine Switzer, I was on the lookout for a chair that shouted 1967. Despite looking quite neat and tidy in the photograph on eBay (along with an artfully placed Penguin Classic), close-up this chair was very shabby and in need of a complete overhaul. However, it did have the advantage of being very groovy. (1)

*Reader, she married him.

1

The Fabric
Photoshop

Now that I had my 1960s two-tone chair I needed some suitably retro fabric. The black and white design was inspired by a pattern I'd seen on some mid-century Danish china. (2)

I found a similar example online and downloaded it. I measured the inside back of the chair (the widest part of the chair) and worked out that 7.8in (20cm) would give me three repeats of the motif exactly. I dragged the downloaded image onto a new canvas sized 7.8 x 17.7in (20 x 45cm)/1181 x 2657/150dpi. (17.7in/45cm would allow me to repeat the motif vertically.)

First, I switched the background color to black and the motif color to white using the Set foreground color/Eyedropper/Paint pot tools. This made the overall design darker. I duplicated the image vertically to make sure that the join was tidy. There was no need to do this horizontally, since there was quite a heavy black margin on the outside edge. I saved the file as 1967 Fabric.jpg and uploaded it to the digital fabric printers. (3)

Note that I used the Repeat style/Drop/ $\frac{1}{3}$ to break-up the vertical lines. There are no hard and fast rules with regards to this: you simply have to play around with the Repeat style and experiment with the pattern on your own designs. (4)

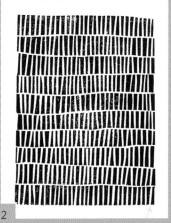

2

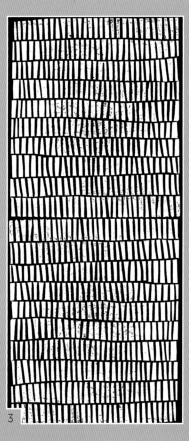

3

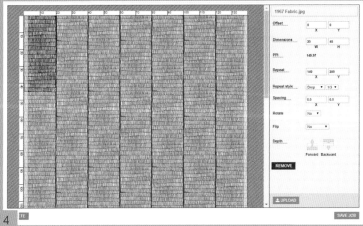

4

85

PROJECT 1967

I decided to print on 100% linen union to add a grainy, vintage look to my 1960s style fabric; the linen was 55in (140cm) wide and 12oz (349 grams).

5

I ordered 8.2ft (2.5m) which was enough to do the chair and at least two cushion backs. (*See* the fabric/quantifying.) (5)

The Katherine Switzer Fabric

The design for the back cushion began with a photograph of Kathrine Switzer being pulled from the track by race organizer Jock Stemple. (6)

I downloaded the image and dragged it to a new canvas sized 21.6 x 16in (55 x 40cm)/3248 x 2362px/150dpi. This was the actual size that I planned to print the cushion front. Then I simply added the different elements layer by layer. For example, the red block of color began as a new canvas sized 4in x 16in (10cm x 40cm), which was colored red using the Set foreground color/Color picker/Paint pot tools and dragged on top of the photo. (7)

The text was typed on a new canvas sized 4 x 16in (10 x 40cm) using the Horizontal type tool and dragged onto the color blocks. (8)

This is the bit that I really enjoy—fiddling and playing around with the layers. Using the Move tool to shuffle and resize the different elements until I get the image just right. (9, 10)

7

8

9

6

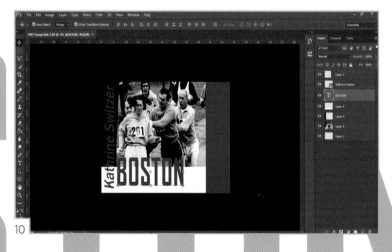

10

Once I was happy with the design, I flattened the image, saved it as Kathrine Fabric.jpg and uploaded it to the online fabric printers. The design was repeated once to give me an extra cushion front. I printed the design on the same linen union fabric as the chair. (11, 12)

Black Fabric
The plain black fabric I used on the arms and outside back was heavy jet black upholstery cotton called Samba by Kobe.

11

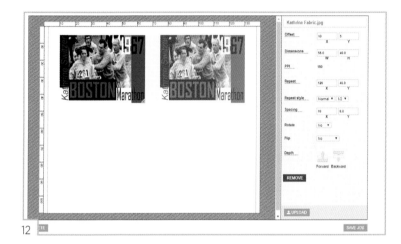
12

The Chair
I started by stripping the chair down to its components: a seat and back (with great springs), two bolt-on plywood arms, and a screw-on metal base. (13–16)

I wanted the upholstery on the chair to be sharp and spare rather than generous and rounded. First the seat and inside back springs were covered over with a layer of tarpaulin or heavy hessian.

13

14

15

16

Inside Back

On the top of the hessian platform on the inside back I glued one layer of 1in (2.5cm) blue (firm seating) foam—just covering the springs, not around the edge of the top or sides. On top of this I glued a

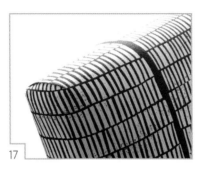

layer of 0.6in (1.5cm) foam that wrapped around the top and sides, finishing on the edge of the frame. (I cut the foam away on the section at the bottom of the sides where the arm would be bolted back on.) Both layers were attached with plenty of spray adhesive on both surfaces.

The corners at the top of the inside back were cut off, and the joins were glued together. Two layers of polyester were glued over the foam to finish. The top fabric was wrapped around the inside back and initially temporary tacked, then stapled, to the outside back of the frame. The corners were finished with a straight fold. (17)

Seat

The seat was upholstered in exactly the same way as was *drawing blood*, except this time I didn't build it up quite so high. Just a 1.9in (5cm) piece of foam was glued over the hessian base, then a 0.6in

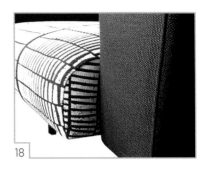

(1.5cm) layer of foam was glued over the top of the seat and front edge. Because the arms bolt on the side of the chair there is no foam down the side of the seat except for a tiny scroll at the very front. The shaping of the front scroll, calico template, and sewing of the top cover were all the same as the seat on *drawing blood*. (18)

Arms

The arms were also upholstered in the same way as *drawing blood*—just square shaped instead of round, and not so chunky. I put only one layer of 1in (2.5cm) foam on the top of the arms and 0.6in (1.5cm) down the sides; very skinny. The calico template of the arms and the sewing of the top cover were the same as the arms on *drawing blood*. (19)

Once the seat/inside back and arms had their top covers stapled down, the arms were bolted back in place. (20)

Outside Back

The outside back was blocked in with calico but any spare strong cloth would do. The black fabric for the outside back was cut in a T-shape, tucked under, pinned in place, and attached with flat black upholstery nails. (21, 22)

Cushion

I made a cushion pad to fit the back of the chair exactly. I always make my own cushion pads using calico remnants and reclaimed polyester that I have teased and shredded to make the stuffing. Using the Kathrine Switzer print as the front, and the black and white fabric as the back, I made a cushion with a finished measurement of 21.6 x 16in (55 x 40cm). It's a cute idea to sew a discreet label of your name in the seam of your cushions. (23–25)

A new black base cloth was tacked to the bottom of the seat in readiness for the metal legs. They had been rubbed down with wire wool, painted with matt black metal paint (Hammerite) and were looking pretty sharp when I screwed them back in place.

Seventeen years after Kathrine's famous Boston Marathon run, she commentated for ABC News on Joan Benoit becoming the first women's Olympic marathon champion.

21

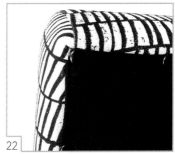

22

23

24

25

murder

Very early one morning I was sitting in my car outside a supermarket just as it was getting light. The parking lot was deserted except for me and at least a dozen jet-black crows squawking and diving, and wheeling and flapping, in an extraordinary menacing dance.

I learned that they are usually rather solitary birds but when they gather it's called a mobbing and that the collective noun for crows is a murder.

The Fabric

There were crows flapping around for quite a while before I had time to get them out of my head and onto a fabric. I had decided that my fabric design would place the birds on one side of the chair and have them emerging from a jumble of murky black into the empty blue sky. (1)

Photoshop

I had also decided to print my design on linen union (55in/140cm wide) to keep the image matt and murky. I already had the chair, so I was able to make the design fit exactly. The vertical measurement of the inside back and the seat was each roughly 31.5in (80cm). My idea was to have the design repeated down the inside back and the seat; roughly matching between the two. The chair was quite narrow so the bird artwork needed to be only 17.7in (45cm) horizontally.

1

I made a new canvas sized 27.5 x 31.5in (70 x 80cm)/4134 x 4724px/150dpi. The canvas was half the width of the fabric (55in/140cm). I planned to make half of the design on this canvas, then duplicate it to the other side on a new canvas 55in (140cm) wide.

The background color was my starting point: I needed to capture the blue/black of the dawn sky. I arrived at the color by first clicking on Set foreground color and Eyedropper tools and sampling the blue from an image of a piece of willow pattern china that I had downloaded. Using the Paint pot tool, I colored the canvas with the blue and made it a few shades darker with a couple of clicks of low opacity black.

I trawled through some bird images online and chose about ten birds that had the right shape and attitude. Some of them weren't crows so I colored them blacker to blend in with the rest of the mob. I cropped out the bird images and dragged them onto my blue canvas: each bird had a separate layer. (2)

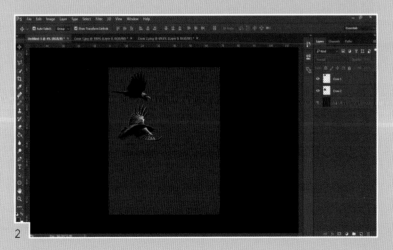

2

PROJECT murder

Now I had to make the murder come to life! Essentially this involved putting black silhouettes of birds underneath lighter, more defined images. Here and there with my digital pen, I highlighted the feathers and made some of the eyes and beaks "pop." It was a long process but well worth my time and patience. I also darkened the areas of blue on the far left (behind and in between the birds) to make it look like they were flying out of the gloom toward the light. (3, 4)

3

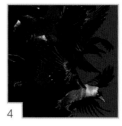
4

5

Once I was happy with my mob of crows I made a new canvas sized 55 x 31.5in (140 x 80cm)/8268 x 4724px/150dpi. I dragged my artwork onto the new canvas. Then I duplicated it, dragged it horizontally, and reversed the image. Finally I used the Offset tool to make sure the pattern repeated vertically. I flattened the image, saved the file as Murder Fabric.jpg, and uploaded it to the online fabric printers. (5, 6)

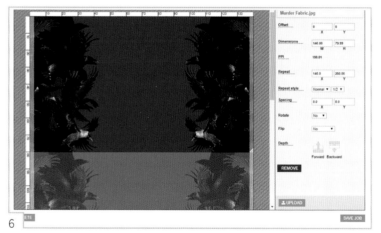
6

I ordered 8.2ft (2.5m) of linen union, which gave me the two repeats I needed (the outside back is cut from the right hand side of the fabric), plus a bit extra for a cushion. When the murder fabric came back from the printers it struck me that the menacing bird motif would adapt well to a bit of chaise longue action. I used the same artwork, this time on satin cotton, to cover the chaise longue pictured on page 2 . . . I will resist the temptation to call it a double murder.

The Chair

I found this dusty old chair loitering at the back of my store and decided that it had the potential to showcase my sinister design. Talent-wise it was able to perform a subtle but impressive reclining action. I've come across a few chairs like this over the years: I think they date back to the utility era during or just after the Second World War. Utility furniture is generally as sound as a pound and well worth reupholstering. (7)

7

The seat was bolted to the back, and the back was bolted to the frame, so I was able to take the whole thing apart: that allowed me to strip down and reupholster the seat and the back away from the frame. While the seat and back were out of the way, I cleaned and sanded the frame. It was utterly transformed by a few coats of black paint and polish. (*See* the frame/finishing.) (8)

Inside Back

The inside back had a piece of plywood as a base for the upholstery which simply needed a new foam pad. I wrapped a 1in (2.5cm) piece of blue (firm seating) foam in a layer of polyester, temporary-tacked it in place and then stapled it home. I cut the fabric for the inside back, with the most prominent bird roughly in the center. It transpired that this striking bird was not a crow, but a jackdaw. As soon as my design went on show in the gallery where I show my stuff, I discovered that everyone's an ornithologist! The fabric was turned under at the edges, temporary tacked and then nailed in place using black-headed gimp pins. (9)

Seat

As is often the case with utility furniture, the seat had a spring unit encased in thick wads of lumpy wool felt. The spring unit was damaged and very shaky, so I decided to dispense with the springs altogether and remodel the seat by using just foam. The metal spring unit was recycled and the wool went into my "shoddy" bag to be used again.

8

9

10

I started by webbing the seat and covering it with a tarpaulin or heavy hessian platform. First to be glued onto the platform was a layer of 1in (2.5cm) 6lb (2.7kg) chip foam, cut to fit the seat frame. On top of this went a layer of 1in (2.5cm) blue (firm seating) foam, cut 1.9in (5cm) smaller than the seat frame all the way around. This smaller piece helps to push up the center of the seat into a slight dome shape.

Next I glued on a piece of 1.9in (5cm) blue foam the exact size of the seat frame. To make the shape of the seat, I glued four panels of calico to the top edges of the foam; front edge, back edge, and both side edges. These panels were pulled down and temporary-tacked to the frame, forming a pleasing domed shape on the seat.

When I was happy with the overall look of the seat, I stapled the calico to the frame. One layer of polyester went over the foam and calico panels. The top cover for the seat was cut to continue the design from the inside back. First the fabric was temporary-tacked under the frame, then stapled home. The front and back corners were finished with a straight fold and secured with a black-headed gimp pin. (*See* the guts/techniques.) I finished the seat by tacking on a black base cloth. (10, 11)

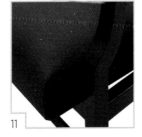

11

Outside Back

The outside back of the chair was a recess in the frame that originally had a piece of tightly fitting fabric-covered cardboard. I thought I could probably improve on that with a piece of really thin (3mm) Foamex (PVC foam sheet), cut to fit very snugly in the recess (I also happened to have a load of offcuts to use, but ordinary stiff cardboard would have worked as well). A layer of polyester was glued to the Foamex.

I cut a piece of fabric with the most prominent bird's head roughly in the center, remembering that the birds were flying the opposite way on the outside back! Using Copydex, I glued the edges of the fabric to the underside of the Foamex. The back of the panel and the recess were liberally sprayed with adhesive, and the panel was carefully pressed into the recess. A black-headed gimp pin was hammered home in each corner. (12)

Last, I took the newly painted bolts and bolted the seat onto the back, and the back onto the chair frame. (13)

Now I could relax in this surprisingly comfortable little recliner and be thankful that the birds had stopped flapping around in my head and flown away. (14)

13

12

14

screen goddesses

I made this screen for International Women's Day, as a celebration of six women and their contribution to women's running:

• Violet Piercy

• Diane Leather

• Julia Chase Brand

• Florence Ilot

• Sarah Attar

• Joan Benoit

Joan Benoit was the first female Olympic Marathon Champion, winning gold at the Los Angeles Olympics in 1984.
On the eve of the anniversary of her first Boston Marathon win, aged 62, she ran with her daughter in 3.04 mins. Beating the over 60's record by 9 minutes.

Sarah Attar was the first female runner to represent Saudi Arabia at the 2012 London Olympics. She ran in defiance of the Saudi clerics ruling that her participation would lead to moral corruption, loss of virginity and lesbianism. However she did have to agree to walk behind her male teammates at the opening ceremony. Wearing the hijab, she finished last in the womens 800m, almost half a minute behind her fellow runners. When Sarah finally crossed the finish line the crowd at the olympic stadium gave her a standing ovation.

I'm a long-distance runner myself, so I have good reason to be grateful to these girls. Thanks to women like them, I've enjoyed the opportunity to take part in many exhilarating competitive races all over the world: through breathtaking countryside, down famous city streets, along coastal paths, and across a few grueling mountain ranges. So far I have run eight marathons and I'm looking forward to my ninth!

I had to cram a lot of information onto each panel to tell their individual stories of determination and chutzpah, but the overall message remains very simple.

"Who run the world? Girls"
– Beyoncé

The women I chose to feature on the screen have individually been on my radar for a long time—some of them I've known about for years but never had the right project to celebrate their achievement. They all have great stories; here's what it says about them on the screen.

97

Diane

In 1955 a talented young chemist named Diane Leather ran a mile in four minutes forty-five seconds. Her record-breaking achievement was recorded as a "world best" rather than "world record," because this distance for women was not recognized for a further fifteen years. Coincidently, at the same time Roger Bannister's four-minute mile was making headlines around the world. He received a knighthood. (1)

Florence

There is an ancient tradition among the staff at the Houses of Parliament in London to attempt to run across Westminster Bridge within the twelve chimes of noon from Big Ben. In 1934, Florence Ilot was the first person on record to achieve this; she was just nineteen at the time and on her lunch break from waitressing at the Commons Tearoom. (2)

Julia

In 1960 a brilliant young zoologist and championship runner named Julia Chase Brand entered the 5-mile Manchester Road Race in her home state of Connecticut, USA. At the time it was not open to women and she was warned that if she continued she would be banned from competitive running for life. Julia lobbied for a year to be allowed to take part officially, but to no avail. So the following year she ran without permission in thirty-three minutes forty seconds, coming in at 128th ahead of ten men. For this she was given a lifetime ban by the governing body unless she agreed to "Stay out of men's races." After a further thirteen years of lobbying, women were finally allowed to take part. Julia ran the race again at the age of sixty-nine—this time officially. (3)

Violet

Violet Piercy is recognized by the International Amateur Athletic Federation (IAAF) as having set the first women's marathon record in 1926 with a time of 3 hours 40 minutes. Again, like Diane, her achievement was recorded as a "world best" rather than a "world record," because women were not officially allowed to compete at this distance for another forty-four years. (4)

4

6

Joan

Joan Benoit was the first female Olympic marathon champion, winning gold at the Los Angeles Olympics in 1984. On the eve of the anniversary of her first Boston Marathon win, aged sixty-two, she ran with her daughter in three hours four minutes, beating the over-60s record by nine minutes. (5)

5

Sarah

Sarah Attar was the first female runner to represent Saudi Arabia at the 2012 London Olympics. She ran in defiance of the Saudi clerics who ruled that her participation would lead to moral corruption, loss of virginity, and lesbianism. However, she was approved to compete but had to agree to walk behind her male teammates at the opening ceremony. Wearing the hijab, she finished last in the women's 800 meters, almost half a minute behind her fellow runners. When Sarah finally crossed the finish line, the crowd at the Olympic stadium gave her a standing ovation. (6)

The Screen

Imagine how overexcited I was when my other half announced that he was going to do a carpentry course. I've always dreamt of having a carpenter on the premises.

The beautiful three-paneled screen he made for my project measured 23.5 x 63in (60 wide x 160cm high), exactly as specified. I planned to keep the style of the project very simple, not covering my fixings with a trimming but showing the nails like an artist's canvas. I started by sanding the little square feet and gave them a couple of coats of black paint, followed by a couple of coats of black wax polish. Then I wrapped them up in calico scraps for protection. I stapled two layers of calico very tightly over each panel to make a firm support for the top fabric. (11, 12)

11

12

13

14

I temporary-tacked the first panel to the frame. (13)

Then I pulled the fabric very tight from top to bottom, repositioning the temporary tacks until the panel was as tight as a drum. Next I made V-shaped cuts around the hinges and pulled the fabric very tightly from side to side and temporary tacked it down. Once I had three panels in place (side-by-side, on one side of the screen), I stapled the panels to the frame and trimmed the fabric close to the staples. (14)

I repeated the process on the remaining three panels, except this time I turned the fabric under and nailed it in place with panel pins (just covering the staples). (15–18)

15

16

How magnificent is Violet Piercy— thundering down the lanes of Old Windsor in shorts and a T-shirt at a time when most women wouldn't have left the house without a hat!

17

18

kathakali

Thanks to globalization, lots of places in the world have similarities with home these days, but India remains bracingly foreign. The astonishing beauty and weirdness of the place still feels distinctly alien—as if you've landed on another planet. Indeed, so many Indians showed up for the Kumph Mela Festival, it could literally be seen from another planet. Shockingly, there are no bin men to collect the rubbish in India, and it gets so cold the goats have to wear jumpers. It's considered lucky to be trampled by a cow, but even luckier to have a coconut smashed on your head—that also brings good health. It's home to four hundred million vegetarians, and every single vegetable that all of those vegetarians eat has been curried. And yes . . . there is a monkey knocking on the window.

1

We arrived back home in February to shocking cold and a mean ration of daylight. I thought I'd better get my impressions of India onto a fabric design quickly before my eyes adjusted to the gloom. (1)

PROJECT kathakali

The Frame and Upholstery

I had a chair frame languishing in my store for about a year that would do very nicely. It had been enthusiastically conceived and knocked together for a project that I eventually decided to abandon: in the end I had to admit that the idea didn't make my heart sing. (*See* the idea/love.)

The frame was constructed in my usual cavewomen style of carpentry. Basically glued and screwed with the addition of strengthening brackets on the legs (which were going to be fabric-covered).

The dimensions were height 28.5in (73cm)/width 26.5in (68cm)/depth 26.5in (68cm)/seat height 16in (40cm)/leg height 12.5in (32cm). The construction of the fame and the upholstery method were exactly the same as for *love me tender*, including the proportions of foam and the style of the top cover. Kathakali was essentially a square version of the little love seat that became *love me tender*. Only the front of the arms was straight instead of curved, which made it an easier frame to upholster. (2)

2

The Fabric

Photoshop

This may look like a complicated design, but it's actually very straightforward and has many similarities to *the stuff*. In essence, it was just a background onto which images were dragged and dropped. This is another example of a design that was tailor-made to fit the chair. I needed approximately 47in (120cm) to run the design vertically down the inside back and seat. Horizontally I needed approximately 27.5in (70cm) to cover the width of the seat. (3)

3

I planned to assemble half of the design on a 13.5in (35cm) wide canvas and duplicate it across the width of the fabric. To start I found a black and white pattern online and downloaded it. (4)

I made a new canvas sized 13.5 x 47in (35 x 120cm)/2067 x 7087px/150dpi.

4

Next I duplicated the black and white image vertically and horizontally to cover the canvas and make the background. (5)

5

For the border I made another new canvas sized 13.5 x 11in (35 x 28cm)/2067 x 1631px/150dpi. I found a polka-dot design (which I recolored) and some old Indian patterns that I turned into a seamless border by using the Offset tool horizontally. I dragged the finished border onto the black and white background. (6, 7)

6

7

Then it was just a case of conjuring up my visual memories of India, sourcing a usable image (cropping) and dragging it onto the black and white background. On our trip we were lucky enough to visit Kerala in Southern India where the traditional Hindu dance entertainment is Kathakali. The character in the center is the main protagonist whose face you see everywhere you go in Kerala. Other elements in my design were papayas, marigolds, monkeys, henna tattoos, humming birds, hummingbird beer, and an elephant. In the grass there is a discarded water bottle and a Coke bottle—just to acknowledge the growing problem of pollution and plastic waste that threatens all of the above. When all the elements were in place, I flattened the layers and saved the image as Artwork.jpg. (8–10)

8

9

10

107

PROJECT kathakali

I made a new canvas sized 59 x 47in (150 x 120cm)/8858 x 7087px/150dpi. To ensure that all the vibrant detail was well replicated I chose to print my design on Panama heavy cotton, 59in (150cm) wide. I dragged the Artwork.jpg onto the right side of the new canvas. Then I duplicated and reversed it to make the first mirror image of the design. I merged those two layers, then duplicated it again. Now my design was repeated across the width of the fabric.

Next I had some tidying up to do to the design. The beer bottle label and the Indian food sign were not symmetrical, so I dragged both of those images onto the design again (in two places) and flattened the layers. I zoomed in close to the joins and using the digital pen I made the fabric seamless. I flattened the image, saved the file as Kathakali Fabric.jpg and uploaded it to the online fabric printers. I worked out that I needed three repeats of the design to get all the motifs on the inside of the chair; that made the order 11.8ft (3.6m) of Panama heavy cotton. That's a lot of fabric for such a small project, but I planned to make some large cushions too. (11, 12)

11

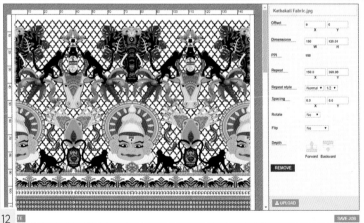

12

The Monkey Fabric

I thought it would be effective to make a simplified version of the main fabric to go on the outside arms and outside back of the chair. I made a new canvas sized 27.5 x 17.7in (70 x 45cm)/4134 x 2657px/150dpi. This was the measurement I needed both for the outside back and outside arm panels. I dragged the black and white background pattern onto the new canvas and duplicated the design to fill the canvas. Then, using the Pen tool, I cropped the red polka-dot section of the border design and dragged that onto the black and white background. Finally, I dragged one of the monkey images onto the design and positioned him on top of the border. I saved the design as Outside Left Fabric.jpg. (13)

13

I made a second new canvas: 27.5 x 17.7in (70 x 45cm) /4134 x 2657px/150dpi. I dragged the file Outside Left Fabric.jpg onto the new canvas and reversed the image; I saved this file as Outside Right Fabric.jpg. Both files were uploaded to the online fabric printers and repeated once. Plus, I ordered an extra repeat of the outside left fabric (for the back of a cushion). I also added a section of the border to my order to ensure that I had enough of the border design for the legs and the cushion backs. This order was also printed on Panama heavy cotton and came to 4.5ft (1.38m). (14)

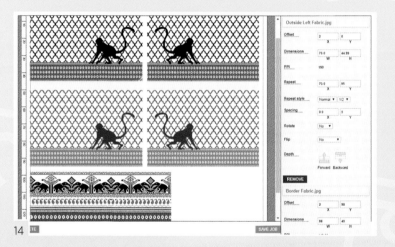

14

Top Cover

Inside Back and Arms

I had to match the top fabric only twice (on the inside of the chair). The inside back had to pattern match the seat exactly. The inside arms fabric had to have matching motifs (a bottle of Kingfisher beer in the middle of each arm). (15, 16)

Outside Back and Arms

Both the outside arms had the monkey facing the same way. The outside back had the monkey on the right-hand side. (17)

Starting with the outside arms, I pinned the panels in place, positioning the monkey in the same place on either side of the chair. (18)

Then I pinned the back panel in place with the monkey on the right. (19)

All the panels were then attached with black-headed gimp pins. (20)

Legs
The border fabric was wrapped around the legs and rails and attached with black-headed gimp pins. (21)

I finished each leg with a dome of silence. To complete the upholstery I put a new black base cloth on the bottom of the seat. (23)

I used silver-colored aluminum embossing sheets to cover the top of the foot rails and to cap the bottom of each leg. These A4 sheets (8.3 x 11.7in/21 x 30cm) feel like very thick tin foil that is pliable and easy to cut with scissors. I attached each piece of aluminum with tiny domed-headed upholstery nails: 3/0 x 10mm nickel on steel—these have a normal-sized shaft but a much smaller head. When all the pieces were nailed in place, I distressed the thin metal to give it a rough appearance with lots of dents. Then I carefully covered the fabric around the outside of the metal with masking tape and painted the aluminum with black metal paint (Hammerite). When it was almost dry, I rubbed it back until I could see the silver metal, with the nail heads and the black paint just sitting in the dents. (22)

I thought the chair would look good with a small back cushion; plus it would be an opportunity to use more of the fabric design. I made a cushion measuring 19.7 x 18in (50 x 46cm) that fitted perfectly and offered a little support to the lumber region. (24)

धन्यवाद और अलविदा अच्छा

microbia

My son and his partner (and Ferris the dachshund) live in Amsterdam, which is good news for me because their apartment is close to Microbia—the only museum in the world devoted to the study of microbes. I designed this fabric long before coronavirus came along and decimated the civilized world, so I understand that the image of anything in a petri dish has taken a bit of a nosedive. Just remember, the vaccine was found lurking in a petri dish too.

It's hard to believe that this zesty fabric depicts some of the nastiest and most deadly diseases known to humanity: botulism, Legionnaires' disease, Ebola, and streptococci, to name just a few.

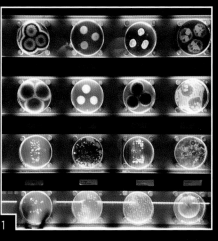

The Fabric

I took a photograph of a wall of petri dishes in the microbe museum. The room was blacked out and the dishes were backlit which made a very striking display and I remember thinking—that's a fabric design right there if ever I saw one. (1)

Photoshop

I started by cropping the most interesting section of the petri dishes from my original photo and dragging it onto a new canvas sized 19.7 x 19.7in (50 x 50cm)/7500 x 7500px/150dpi. I used the Set foreground color/ Color picker/Paint pot tools to make most of the background black, and generally lightened and brightened the colors in the dishes. (2)

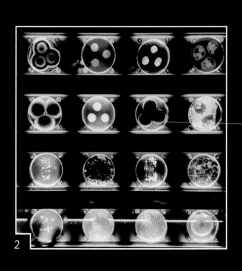

I decided to crop out the less distinct dishes on the bottom row, changing the canvas size to: 19.7 x 14.7in (50 x 37.5cm)/2953 x 2215px/150dpi. I called this File 1. The design was taking shape but needed a greater variety of color and interest, so I searched the internet and downloaded about six more petri dishes of diseases. Then I duplicated File 1 so that I had Files 2, 3, and 4 as well.

I cropped out the new petri dish images, then dragged and dropped them randomly onto the four new files (covering the original, less vibrant petri dishes). I flipped the files horizontally and vertically to make them all look different. With the addition of blue and green microbes the design was beginning to look like a collection of precious jewels or a fruit machine—depending how you look at it. (3-6)

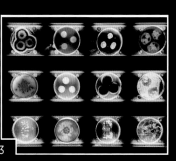
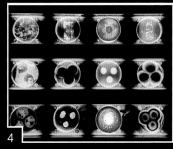
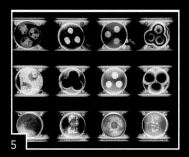
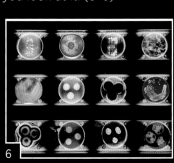

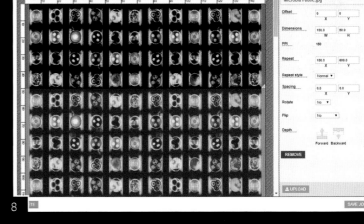

Now I was ready to make the final fabric image for printing. At this point I decided to flip the whole design from horizontal to vertical; I thought the broken lines framing the dishes would look better running down the design. I planned to use Panama heavy cotton, my usual choice of fabric for clarity of print, which is 59in (150cm) wide and 310gsm (9oz/sq yd).

I made a new canvas sized 59in x 19.7in (150 x 50cm) /8858 x2953px/150dpi. I dragged File 1 onto the canvas and flipped it from horizontal to vertical. Then I did the same with Files 2, 3, and 4. I flattened the image, saved the file as Microbia Fabric.jpg and uploaded it to the online fabric printers. I estimated I would need 4.9ft (1.50m) per chair, so 19.7ft (6m) in total. (*See* the fabric/ quantifying.) (7, 8)

Fabric Under the Cushions

For this project I decided it would be fun to make a hidden feature of the cloth that covers the tension springs under the cushions. I always cover tension springs because it makes a neat finish to the job and helps to protect the cushion cover from rubbing on the springs.

I made a copy of the file Microbia Fabric.jpg. Using the Set foreground color and Eyedropper tools, I sampled a color from one of the petri dishes and with the Paint pot tool changed the background from black to acid yellow—it was as simple as that. I then saved the file as Microbia Acid Fabric.jpg and uploaded it to the online fabric printers. I ordered 11.5ft (3.5m) on Panama heavy cotton, which was enough to do all the spring covers and, I hoped a couple of cushions. (9, 10)

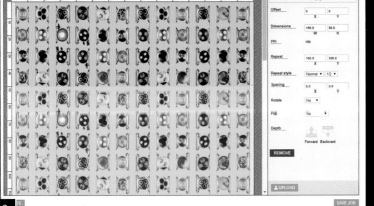

The Chairs

I have had these four chairs in my store for so long I'm not sure where they came from, but I remember they cost peanuts and were a very cute, solid set of frames. I've always called these "school library" chairs because that's where I imagine most of them started life. I suppose they could just as easily be called "unemployment office" chairs or even "prison visitor" chairs—they were popular with the government for their comfort and resilience. (11)

This is the third of four Parker Knoll projects in the book, along with *catfish, test card*, and *double helix*. The upholstery, top cover, and construction of seat and cushion are the same as the other Parker Knolls and are fully explained in *catfish*.

Top Cover

Microbia was a linear design that had to match in three places: inside back to seat cushion, inside back to outside back, seat cushion to front edge. I decided that I would follow the lines of the design and not try to match the petri dishes exactly.

The most important thing with this set of chairs was getting the design in exactly the same place on all four inside backs. (12)

Once I had gotten the inside back correctly positioned, the outside back, cushion, and front edge just followed the line of the petri dishes. (13, 14)

I managed to fit a row of petri dishes on the cushion panels. (15)

13

14

11

12

15

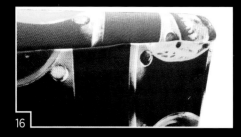

16

The outside back was attached with black-headed gimp pins. (16)

While still in the grip of microbe mania, I covered an old Lloyd Loom ottoman in *microbia* and lined it with the acid yellow version of the design that I had used under the cushions. It was so easy to change the color of the design that I had a meter of white printed as well to make another cushion. Together, the chairs, cushions, and ottoman made a nice collection in the gallery where I sell my work. (17-18)

17

The scariest thing I saw in the microbe museum wasn't—as you might imagine—a deadly virus or microscopic monster, but a cabinet of rotting food. The exhibit was designed to show how long it took for everyday groceries to decompose, and how that looked. No surprises with the fruit and vegetables, but an unwrapped microwave cheese burger that was clearly so full of chemicals it still looked like an edible snack after four years—that was the shocker!

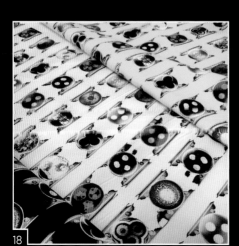

18

mongolian

I once saw a photograph of a man disappearing into an enormous chair shaped like a fur ball; just his feet and hands were left poking out. How could I not have a go at that?

The Frame

The *mongolian* started out as a standard issue, grubby, corduroy swivel chair with two squashy buttoned-back cushions and a (missing) seat cushion. (1)

I started by stripping off all the old upholstery back to the shell. There was a wooden panel set into the seat and one under the shell where the metal swivel base was attached; thankfully, both of these were in good order. (2)

1

2

PROJECT mongolian

The idea was to build up the polyurethane shell so that it resembled the shape of a ball cut in half. I thought that expanding foam would be compatible with the base material of the shell. Expanding foam is a wonderful product, used mainly by builders to fill large cracks, but it also works extremely well as a sculpting material. Be warned—it's crazy stuff! The liquid foam shoots straight out of the can like squirty cream, sticks to everything it touches (don't get it on your hands), and sets like honeycomb concrete. When it dries hard it can easily be sculpted into any shape by using a sharp carving knife; I used it to sculpt a sheep that lives in our garden. It works best if it is built up in layers, letting each layer dry before adding the next. (3)

Before I got going with the expanding foam, I hammered about a dozen kebab sticks (you could use bamboo skewers) into the top edge of the arms, and trimmed them to the new height and shape. That gave me a guide to work to and added a bit of support while the foam was drying. I also squirted some foam down the line between the inside back and inside arm to round-off the inside of the chair as well as the outside. (4)

Next I glued chunks of 6lb (2.7kg) chip foam all the way around the rim of the frame to continue to build-up the circular shape. I sculpted the chip foam into shape using a carving knife. (5)

3

4

5

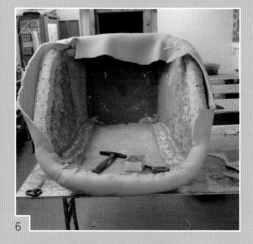

6

7

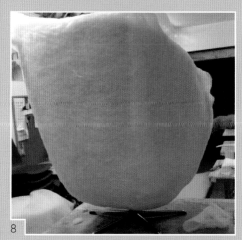

8

The Upholstery

I started the upholstery by drawing a line down the outside back of the shell with marker pen. A layer of 0.6in (1.5cm) blue (firm seating) foam was cut in two pieces; one large middle piece (also marked with a center line) and one front panel, to complete the circumferance of the shell. I matched the centerlines to the centerline on the shell and glued both pieces of foam in place, using spray adhesive. I trimmed and glued the foam together where it met. (6)

It's worth pointing out how important it is to use plenty of spray adhesive on both surfaces to be glued. If you stint on glue at this stage, all the layers will feel as if they are coming away from the shell. To finish the outside back I glued two layers of polyester on top of the foam. (7, 8)

9

10

11

The inside of the shell was covered in 1.9in (5cm) blue foam in the same way as the outside back; this time in three sections. I started by drawing a line with a marker pen down the center of the inside back (tricky now that everything is circular). Then I cut a piece of foam the width and height of the inside back and drew a line down the center. Matching the lines together I firmly glued it in place. Next I cut two pieces of foam big enough to cover the remaining inside arm and front edge and glued them in place. Where the three pieces met, I trimmed them to fit snugly in the shell, then I glued the edges together. To complete the "ball" of foam, I glued all the inside pieces of foam to all the outside pieces of foam, along the top edge of the shell. Finally, two layers of polyester were glued over the top to finish the upholstery. (9–11)

Template

To make the top cover, I first needed to make a calico template of the chair. Believe it or not, the method for covering an egg is basically the same as the method for covering a conventional armchair. I use the same technique to construct all my templates (even the round ones). There is a detailed description of the process in *drawing blood/lovely ovaries*.

First, I checked that the centerline on the foam/polyester was accurate and clear. Then I cut a piece of calico the width and height of the inside back, plus a piece the width and height of the outside back, plus a seam allowance (about 1.9in/5cm to pin the shape; this will be trimmed back to 0.6in/1.5cm). I folded them both in half, cut a notch top and bottom, and drew a line between the two notches.

Then I laid the centerlines of the calico pieces carefully over the center lines on the foam and held them in place with a few anchoring pins. Next I cut a piece of calico the height and width of the inside arm, and the same for the outside arm. I wrote on each piece of calico what it was (inside back, outside back, etc.) and an arrow pointing to the top of the shell at right angles to the floor.

Basically, this template has two long seams that meet at a crossroads. The first seam starts at the center of the inside back (remember, we are dealing with only half of the shell) and runs around the top edge of the chair, finishing in the middle of the front edge. The second seam starts where the inside back meets the seat and runs over the top of the arm, to finish under the seat, where the swivel base is mounted. A few temporary tacks in the wooden seat and wooden base panels helped to hold the calico tightly in place while the seams were being pinned. When both the seams were in place, I had to add a couple of darts to the underside of the template to eliminate the remaining fullness in the calico. (12, 13)

12

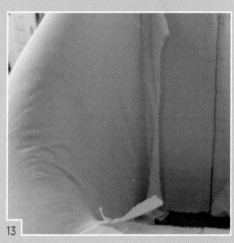

13

Once the pinning was perfect and the template felt very smooth and tight on the foam, out came the anchoring pins and off came the template, leaving just the seam pins in place. I trimmed the seams to 0.6in (1.5cm) and added several random notches to help with the reassembling of the pattern pieces. Then I folded the inside back piece in half and cut the mirror image of the calico in the other side—not forgetting to snip in the notches. I did exactly the same with the outside back calico pattern piece. Now I had four beautiful calico template pieces labeled inside back, outside back, inside arm, and outside arm ready to use as a pattern to cut the top fabric.

Cutting Out

Mongolian got its name from the long-haired faux fur that I used for the cover. There's good news and bad news regarding the use of long-haired fabric. On one hand it's so dense and fluffy it could potentially hide a multitude of sewing sins. However, on the other hand, it will clog up your sewing machine and the cutting process will bless your workshop with gray fluff for weeks to come.

> *Note: When using faux fur, I usually cut the fabric pieces upside down so that the pile of the fur sticks out from the chair, rather than lying flat.*

I pinned the calico pattern pieces onto the fabric, making sure they were all lying in the same direction (the arrows on the pattern pieces help with this). It's always a mistake to turn a pattern piece sideways on faux fur. When I had cut out all the pieces, I pinned them together, matching the notches, and machine-sewed all the seams back together (not forgetting the darts at the base of the cover). At the crossroads on both sides where all four of the pieces meet (inside back, outside back, inside arm, outside arm), I had to stop and reverse the sewing machine four times. I was careful to double-check my sewing—it's easy to leave a tiny hole. Before I put the cover on the shell, I unscrewed the swivel base so that I could temporary-tack the cover to the wooden base panel.

Top Cover

I put the fur cover carefully on the shell (making sure the center marks lined up) and temporary-tacked the fabric to the wooden seat panel and the wooden baseplate. (14)

When all was splendid, I stapled it home. Then, using a curved needle and some strong thread, I brought the front edges of the outside arms closer together at the front of the shell and down toward the base, with long, lacing stitches (like tightening a bodice). These stitches will pull the cover tighter around the frame.

Front Panel

I cut a piece of fur slightly wider than the seat and long enough to reach from the wooden seat panel to the wooden base panel. The top edge of this piece of fur was stapled to the front edge of the wood panel on the seat (this will be under the cushion). Then it was tucked under down the length on both sides, pulled very tight, and stapled to the wooden base panel (hiding the "bodice" stitches underneath). (15)

14

15

Seat Cushion

To make the seat cushion I experimented with various thicknesses of foam to see what would work best. Obviously it had to be comfortable, but at the same time not so perky that it spoiled the hollowed-out shape of the chair. A circular piece of 3in (8cm) deep foam was the answer.

I covered the foam with a piece of fur—just lightly gluing the fabric to the underside of the foam with fabric glue (Copydex)—then I glued it in place on the chair with spray adhesive. Be very careful not to get glue everywhere when doing this! Using a curved needle and strong thread, I hand-sewed the cushion to the chair around its outside edge (twice around for extra strength). Because I had used such long-haired fabric, the cushion disappeared into the shagginess of the seat and wasn't noticeable as a separate piece. (16)

Buttons

My remodeled eggshell no longer had buttoned back cushions, so I had to put a set of covered buttons through the back to keep the cover tight against the inside back. Usually these buttons are placed approximately 11.8in (30cm) from the top of the shell, and either side of the inside back.

First, I made four fluffy 1.1in (29mm) cover buttons. Using a long mattress needle and strong buttoning twine, I threaded up a button and pulled the needle straight through the polyurethane shell. Both buttons were pulled tight and tied off, with the second button on the outside back. (17)

Finally, the polished chrome swivel base was screwed back onto the wooden base panel and I disappeared into the *mongolian*. (18)

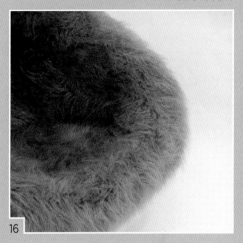

16

17

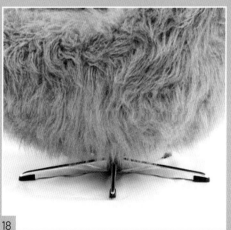

18

double helix

The *double helix* chairs are my small tribute to a brilliant young female scientist. Rosalind Franklin was the British molecular biologist who was responsible for the x-ray photography that led to our understanding of the structure of DNA: photo 51.

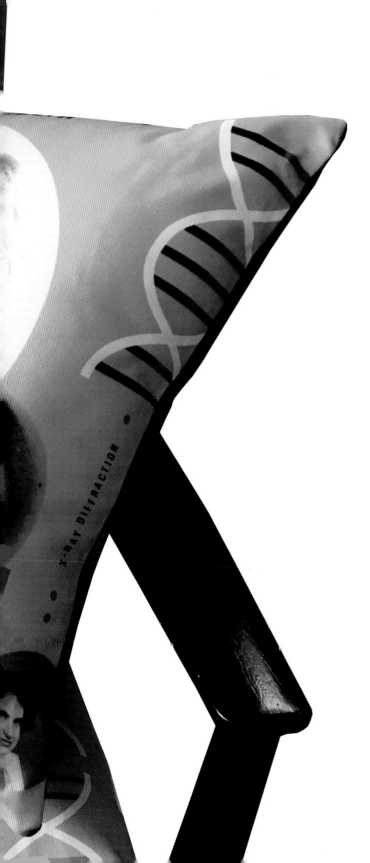

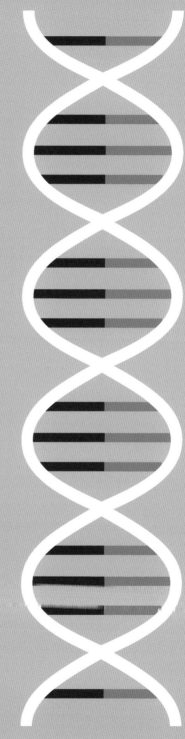

X-RAY DIFFRACTION

2127

The Double Helix

Rosalind made her discoveries at King's College, London, during the early 1950s, when it was extremely hard for women to make a career and gain recognition in science. At the time, only men were allowed to use the university dining room, and after hours her colleagues went to men-only pubs to discuss their work. Rosalind and her team were very close to solving the structure of DNA when one of her colleagues, Maurice Wilkins, showed photo 51 to Francis Crick and James Watson who were part of a rival research team. When they saw the image the puzzle was solved, and they immediately published their results. Crick, Watson, and Wilkins went on to receive the Nobel Prize for the discovery of DNA in 1962. Tragically, Rosalind died of ovarian cancer in 1958, at the age of only thirty-seven. Nobel Prizes are not awarded posthumously, which is just as well, because the boys had no plans to share it.

Once I had the double helix image as the basis for a design, I obviously had to find a suitable pair of chairs. I already had one of these armchairs in my store and a quick sweep of eBay produced number two—a perfect match! (1, 2)

The Chairs

You may have noticed by now that Parker Knoll fireside armchairs are a perennial favorite of mine. This is the last of four Parker Knoll projects in the book: along with *catfish*, *test card*, and *microbia*. The upholstery, top cover, and construction of the seat are the same as the other Parker Knolls and are fully explained in *catfish*.

1

2

3

The Fabric
Photoshop

I started by searching the internet for images of Rosalind and found a series of free-to-download educational posters that were designed by Amanda Phingbodhipakkiya for the Science not Silence campaign. It was a beautiful piece of artwork that contained all of the elements that I needed to tell the story: the photo 51 image, DNA, and Rosalind at her microscope. Plus the colors and the style of the poster reminded me of the 1951 Festival of Britain. I thought that if I cropped a square section of the poster, it would make a great cushion front, and then I could snitch the double helix motif to make a fabric for the chairs. (3)

Cushion Fabric

I downloaded the poster image. Using the Pen tool, I cropped the original image to a square cushion front 19.7 x 19.7in (50 x 50cm) and dragged it to a new canvas sized 19.7 x 19.7in (50 x 50cm)/2953 x 2953px/150dpi. Then I flattened the image, saved it as Helix Cushion Fabric.jpg and uploaded it to the online fabric printers. I decided to print both designs on 59in (150cm) wide Panama heavy cotton. (4, 5)

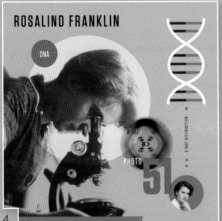

4

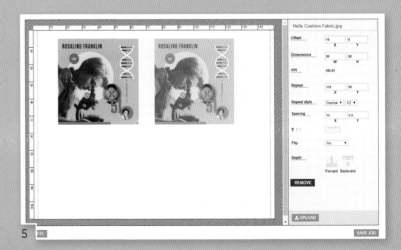

5

Chair Fabric

The widest part of the chairs was 23.5in (60cm) across the inside back. I wanted to place a motif in the middle of the inside back and have at least two repeats either side; that worked out at 5 x 4.7in (12cm) motifs horizontally. Proportionally that made the vertical measurement 7in (18cm). I went back to the original poster image and again using the Pen tool I cropped out the double helix motif and dragged it onto a new canvas sized 4.7 x 7in (12 x 18cm)/709 x 1093px/150dpi. (6)

Then using the Set foreground color tool and the Eyedropper, I sampled the yellow from the original poster to paint the background with the Paint pot tool. I flattened the image, saved it as Double Helix Fabric.jpg, and uploaded it to the digital online fabric printers. (7)

To stagger the repeat of the motif, I used the Repeat style/Drop/½. The order was 16.4ft (5m) allowing 8.2ft/2.5m per chair, to be printed on Panama heavy cotton to match the cushion. (*See* the fabric/ quantifying.) (8, 9)

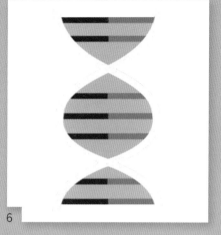
6

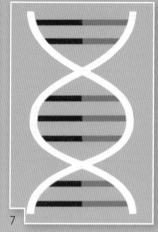
7

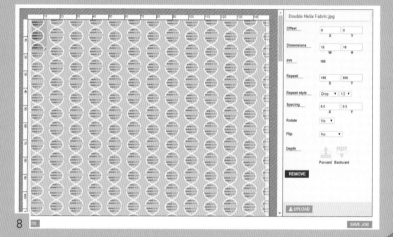
8

9

Top Cover

The double helix fabric had a linear design that I wanted to match in two places: inside back to seat cushion and inside back to outside back. (10)

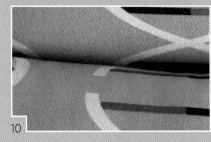

10

Rather than a box-shaped cushion cover with a panel, I gave the seat cushions a single seam at either side and a vertical seam at each corner to make the "box" shape. (11)

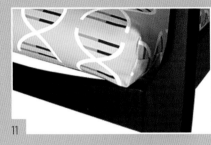

11

The outside back was attached with black-headed gimp pins (12).

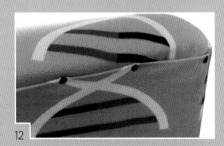

12

Cushions

To accompany the chairs, I made the Rosalind Franklin fabric into a pair of cushions measuring 22.7 x 19.6in (58 x 50cm). I thought it would look good to add a row of double helix motifs from the main fabric to the outside edge of each cushion. I used plain black canvas for the backs of the cushions and a black zipper.

In his memoir *The Double Helix*, James Watson makes no attempt to hide his attitude toward Franklin, whom he admits he tended to dismiss. Rosalind is referred to throughout his book as Rosy—a name she never used.

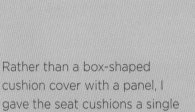

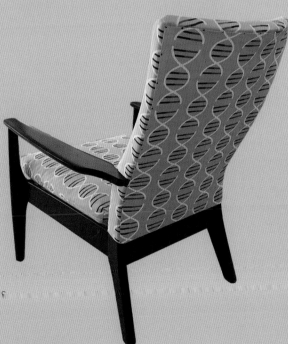

do the math

From a family of reasonably intelligent, somewhat creative people emerges my nephew Roy—a mathematical genius. I heard that he had given his mother a mathematical formula proving that she was always right (now framed). (1)

Was it possible to expand on this theme I asked—surely there's a greater truth to be proven? Eventually Roy produced a beautiful long sum demonstrating in pure mathematics that women are more often right than men. Genius.

1

The Frame

Now that I was in possession of this controversial calculation (on a disappointingly grubby scrap of paper) I began casting around for a suitably absurd chair that would be equal to its message. Something modern and boxy—possibly with an odd shape? (2)

At the same time, I was beginning to get tired of skinning my shins on a Queen Anne reproduction wing chair that was taking up space in my workshop. Could that be the answer? (3)

The frame was as solid as a rock and robust enough to withstand some radical surgery. It had a lovely broad seat and generous open arms, but the rest would have to go. I stripped the chair down to the frame, saving all the calico, wool felt, and polyester to reuse. The old top cover went to the local dump to be recycled.

I began the transformation by sawing off the wings and the top rail of the inside back. A good height for the back of a boxy chair is around 29.5in (75cm), so I glued and screwed a new top rail across the inside back at that height; straight rather than arched. Then I used a saw to square off the wooden scrolls on the front of the arms. The back legs were a fairly inoffensive

square shape, but the front legs were definitely not part of the plan.

I sawed off the two Queen Anne style front legs. Luckily, there was a good solid piece of wood for me to screw in a new pair of straight legs (made by my lovely husband). To fit the legs I drilled two holes (the size of the center pin on the new legs), hammered in two Tee nuts, and screwed the front legs in place. The original back legs were sanded back to bare wood and all four legs were stained with a combination of mahogany and a warmer cherry color. I finished them with three coats of dark oak wax polish and hammered a dome of silence into the bottom of each leg.

2

3

133

The Fabric

Having decided to celebrate Roy's arithmetic, I had to work out how best to splash it all over the chair.

Photoshop

Do the math is another good example of a tailor-made fabric. I decided that a simple, playful design would work well with the chair and set the right tone to convey the information. I wanted to present the complete sum on all the panels of the top cover: inside back, seat, outside back, inside arm, and outside arm. That meant I had to make the sum motif fit on the smallest panel, which was the inside back, its widest horizontal measurement being 31.5in (80cm). A sum motif measuring 23.5 x 23.5in (60 x 60cm) fitted comfortably on the inside back. I designed the artwork to have a 23.5 x 23.5in (60 x 60cm) motif set within an 31.5in x 31.5in (80 x 80cm) design repeat.

I started by downloading a simple circle design. Then made a new canvas sized 16 x 16in (40 x 40cm)/2362 x 2362px/150dpi. I used the Move tool to drag the image onto the new canvas and made it fit. Then, using the Set foreground color/Color picker/Paint pot tools, I colored the background black and the circles white. (4, 5)

I made another new canvas: 31.5 x 31.5in (80 x 80cm)/4724 x 4724px/150dpi. Then I dragged the image onto the top-left corner. I duplicated the image three more times, horizontally and vertically, to fill the new canvas (tidying up the joins as I went with the digital pen). (6)

Now I had an image that was the right scale and size. Using the digital pen, I wrote the mathematical formula in the white circles, in the center of the design. (7)

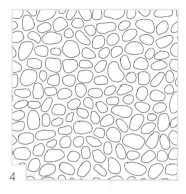
4

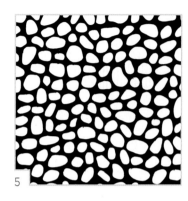
5

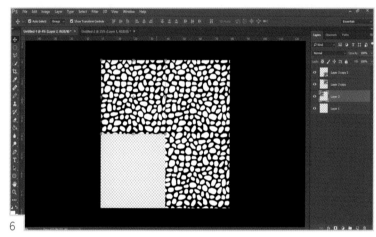
6

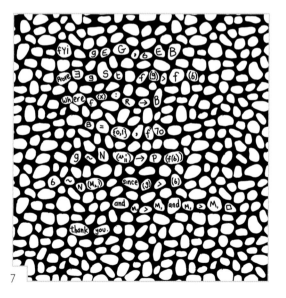
7

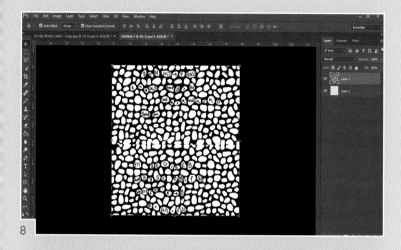

8

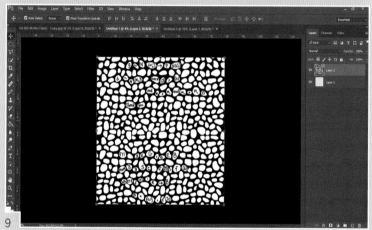

9

Then, using the Offset tool, I made sure my design would repeat seamlessly as a fabric vertically and horizontally. (8, 9)

I flattened the image, saved it as Do the Math Fabric.jpg and uploaded it to the online fabric printers. I chose to print the design on 55in (140cm) linen union to give it a slightly grainy quality. I had to center the mathematical motif in seven places on the chair so I ordered 13ft (4m) of fabric, which gave me eight repeats of the motif to play with. (*See* the fabric/quantifying) (10, 11)

The Upholstery

The top cover on this chair exactly mirrors the joins in the foam and the seams in the calico template underneath, so I'm going to illustrate the process with lots of images of the finished cover. First, I clearly marked the center of the chair at the top and bottom of the outside back. Then I made a platform for the new foam by blocking in the inside back, inside arms, seat, outside arms, and outside back with webbing and heavy hessian (leaving the bottom of the outside arms and outside back temporary tacked).

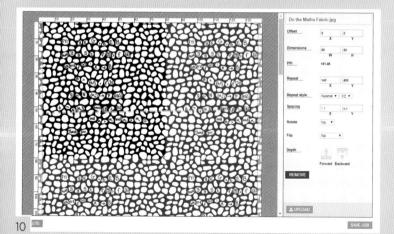

10

11

Seat

The seat was built from a 4in (10cm) piece of blue (firm seating) foam with a centerline, cut to fit the T-shape of the seat frame and glued in place with spray adhesive. I could have used layers of foam to build up the seat, but I just happened to have a 4in (10cm) piece in stock. Over the top of this (matching center lines) I glued a layer of 1in (2.5cm) foam cut long enough and wide enough to cover the front and side edge of the seat. The foam front corners (above the front legs) were cut off and the edges were glued together. (12)

12

Arms

I glued a section of squared-off 6lb (2.7k) chip foam to the top of the arms in the same way as the arms in *drawing blood*. Over the chip foam I glued a 1.9in (5cm) layer of foam that covered the inside arms and the top of the arms. Then, a 1.9in (5cm) layer of foam was glued to the outside arms and wrapped around (what used to be the front scroll) to meet the foam on the inside arms. (13)

The join between the foam on the inside arms and outside arms was glued and strips of polyester were glued over the joins. (14, 15)

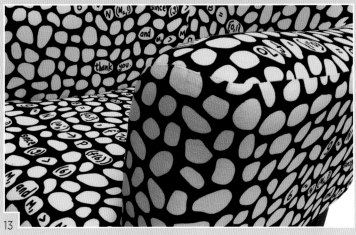

13

14

15

Inside Back

For the inside back I cut and glued a piece of 1in (2.5cm) foam to fit the shape of the inside back. Over the top of that, I glued a 1.9in (5cm) layer of foam the same shape at the bottom, but big enough at the top to wrap around the sides and top of the inside back. Both layers of foam had center lines that matched with the center marks on the chair. The corners at the top of the inside back were chopped off and a straight join was glued together. (16)

The joins between inside back and inside arms were glued together and strips of polyester were glued over the joins. (17, 18)

Outside Back

Finally, I cut and glued in place a piece of 0.6in (1.5cm) foam to cover the outside back, matching the centerline to the center marks. I glued the edges of the outside back to the inside back and outside arms and glued strips of polyester over the joins. Now the whole of the inside and outside of the frame was encased in foam. (19, 20)

16

19

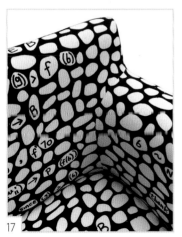

17

18

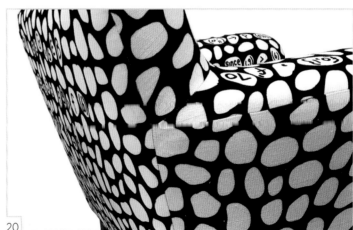

20

Template

Regardless of its shape or complexity, the technique for making a calico template is the same for every chair. (*See drawing blood/lovely ovaries.*)

The template for this chair was made as a single piece of sewing that exactly followed the same lines as the foam joins underneath. It comprised an inside back, outside back, one inside arm, and one outside arm (the seat didn't need a template). Remember, you make a template of only half the chair.

I cut out the calico pieces, plus generous turnings (1.9in/5cm for pinning, which will be trimmed to 0.6in/1.5cm). The inside back, and outside back pieces were folded lengthways, a notch was snipped top and bottom, and a centerline was drawn from notch to notch.

I checked that the centerlines on the inside back, and outside back of the foam were accurate. Then I matched the line down the middle of the foam to the line down the middle of the central calico pieces and held them in place on the chair with a few anchoring pins. I anchor-pinned the inside arm, and outside arm calico pieces to the chair and drew on each pattern piece what it was (inside arm, outside back, etc.), plus an arrow pointing to the top of the chair at right angles to the floor. Then I got busy pinning the seams in place.

This was quite a complicated piece of sewing with lots of seams and junctions that had to echo exactly the foam joins underneath. (21)

> *Note: I cannot emphasize enough how important it is to take your time getting the seams exactly right on a calico template—a rushed, badly fitting template will make a badly fitting top cover. Sorting that out will ultimately waste more of your time!*

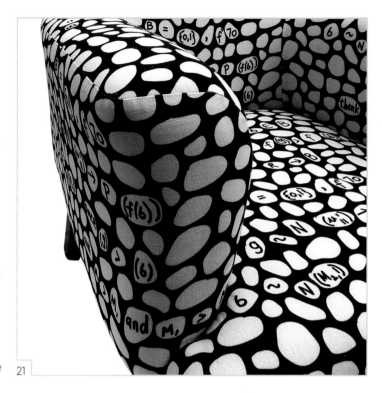

21

Once all the seams were in place (and looking good!), I took out the anchoring pins and carefully lifted the template off the chair. Then I trimmed the seams to 0.6in (1.5cm) and snipped in a few random notches to help match the pattern pieces back together again. I folded the inside back, and outside back pieces in half, and cut a mirror image of the shape (plus notches). Then I cut a calico copy of the inside back, and outside back, and two copies of the inside arm, and outside arm.

The original calico template pieces were used as a pattern to cut the top fabric. The set of calico copies (which made a complete cover) were sewn together and tightly fitted over the foam, temporary tacked first, then stapled in place (leaving the outside arms and outside back temporary tacked for now). One layer of polyester went over the top of the calico before the top cover.

Top Cover

First, I cut the top cover for the seat by measuring the width and depth required (with the sum motif in the center). The seat corners were finished with a single straight fold and secured with a black gimp pin. (*See* the guts/Cutting a Front Leg.) (22)

By carefully placing the calico pattern pieces on the top fabric I was able to center the motif on each of the remaining panels of the chair. My aim was to feature Roy's sum in its entirety on the inside back, outside back, inside arms and outside arms. (23)

When all the remaining pattern pieces were cut out, I matched the notches, pinned them, then machine-sewed them together. With a piece of sewing like this, it's sensible to run all the seams through the machine twice. Now I was ready to put the gorgeous, perfectly fitting black and white linen cover onto the chair: temporary-tack it in place, then staple all the layers home.

To finish, I tacked a new black base cloth to the bottom of the seat and called my adorable nephew Roy to apologize for wrecking his career.

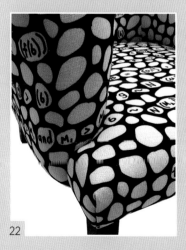

22

23

the frame
the guts
the fabric
and
the wrinkles

the frame

A good frame is the bones of an idea. With just the addition of a few simple materials it has the potential to be sculpted into whatever shape you can imagine. I hope some of my projects will have shown you that.

finding

Free!

First make sure that everyone knows that you renovate furniture and that you are interested in their castoffs. Nowadays we are all getting queasy about tipping stuff into the garbage, so you will be doing your friends a favor, and I promise more treasure than trash will come your way. This is how I came by some of my favorite projects.

Secondhand

I'm sure there are plenty of places online where you can find cheap second-hand projects, but the three I use are eBay, Facebook Market Place, and Gumtree. If you see something you like on a listing, contact the seller straight away and make a reasonable offer. They may not accept it at first, but all sellers like to know they have a buyer in their back pocket and very often they will get back to you. If you see something you really love, don't dither about; pay the price and get it!

If the object of your love is for sale only in an online auction, it's still worth contacting the seller and making your offer. Legend has it that there are tricks that will help you be the winning bid on eBay—sadly, I'm not part of that magic circle, and I too have been thwarted on many occasions.

It's also well worth keeping an eye on your local auction house. Once or twice I've bought furniture at auction and quite often these days you can view and bid online. Finally, it's worth remembering that you regret only the chairs that you *didn't* buy—I'm haunted by the stuff that got away.

THE FRAME
building

I think by now I've demonstrated quite clearly that I'm not a carpenter, though I've never allowed that to dampen my enthusiasm for carpentry. If I have a vision of a frame that I can't find elsewhere, I make it. I don't intend to explain my "cavewoman" carpentry techniques here; that would be silly. But I would like to pass on some words of encouragement and caution.

As you progress through your upholstery projects, you'll soon get a feel for what makes a good frame and how they are put together. The appropriate height of a seat, the width of an inside back, and where the upholstery rails should be placed—all these details will become familiar to you. Let go of the idea that you are somehow competing with Messrs. Chippendale and Hepplewhite and have a go!

Finally, a word of caution

We all know what happens to a chair once it's out in the big bad world: abuse is not too strong a word. So, once you've hammered, sawed, bashed, crashed, glued, and screwed your frame together, put it through a thorough strength test in the workshop; that is definitely the place to find out if it has any weaknesses.

chameleon

This is a typical frame-building story. I dragged an enormous pile of brightly colored cotton fabrics home from Sri Lanka, planning to make a collection of multicolored furniture. For the first piece I pictured a tiny, leggy sofa, upholstered with all the coral, pink, and orange fabrics. At the time I didn't have a frame that was anything like that in my store, nor could I find what I was looking for online, and then, by an extraordinary stroke of luck, these dainty legs waved to me from a skip. When we met, they were attached to a broken armchair, but very soon they became part of my vision of a weenie two-seater. As you can see in the photograph (on page 142), there's some fairly unorthodox carpentry going on there, but it turned out to be an incredibly robust little frame that is still going strong after five years. I could have sold *chameleon* ten times over. (1–3)

1

2

3

finishing

Paint

On the subject of painting in general, I know from my teaching days that painting furniture is one of those skills that everyone thinks they have, but most people don't. That may sound harsh but believe me, I've seen some shocking paint jobs in my time. The reality is that there are no shortcuts if you want a good finish that will enhance your design. A hasty paint job is a total waste of effort.

It won't have escaped your notice that I paint a good deal of my furniture—and invariably the color I choose is black; there are some very good reasons for that.

First, a lot of the chairs that I upholster are in bad shape by the time I get to them. A frame might be very solid but the show wood could be stained by exposure to weather, mold, and rust. It's a skilled and time-consuming job to properly restore wood that has been damaged in that way; I would prefer to make a good job of covering it with paint.

Also, I often work with utility furniture that was originally stained and varnished in a factory spray booth and was never intended to be stripped down and exposed.

You can waste a lot of time sanding down a chair that is made of marked, mismatched wood that was never meant to be on show or, as in the case of *double helix*, a pair of chairs that matched in every way but were made from different wood.

Second, I use a lot of strong colors in my fabric and my designs almost always look better against a black frame. There's something about black that makes my fabric pop. (4-6)

Note: One last thing before we dive into the paint pot—a note of caution. The frames I paint are drawn exclusively from the last chance saloon. They have no antique or historical value and are, without exception, mass-produced. Be careful not to affect the value of something old or rare by painting it.

7

10

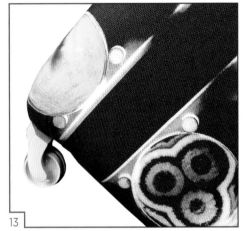

13

8

11

14

9

12

15

My Black Paint Treatment

Materials

7a. Multicoat/semigloss topcoat and primer/black—I use Hempel marine paint.

7b. Thinners No. 1

7c. Fine 00-0 steel wool

7d. Black furniture polish with beeswax. I use a German wax called Delara.

Method

i. Start by cleaning the frame with a damp cloth to remove all the dirt. If you're working around old existing upholstery, wrap it up, or cover it to make sure it can't shed dust onto your paintwork.

ii. Lightly sand the areas to be painted, and then wipe them clean again with a cloth made damp with white spirit. Then, using a clean, dry paint brush, flick the dust out of the corners and crevices.

iii. In a screw top jar, mix approximately 8.5fl oz (250ml) of Multicoat black paint with approximately 1.7fl oz (50ml) Thinners No. 1. Mix it well with a stick, or screw the lid on tightly and give it a good shake (emphasis on the word tightly). It should be quite a thin consistency, like single cream.

iv. Using a new 1in (2.5cm) paintbrush, paint the wood sparingly with the mix.

v. When the paint has dried, rub it well into the grain with the fine wire wool. First wipe the sanding dust off the wood with a rag, then wipe it over with a clean cloth made damp with the white spirit.

vi. Repeat the painting and rubbing-down process four times. Continue to use the clean dry paintbrush to flick the sanding dust out of the corners and crevices before applying the next coat. By slowly building up thin coats of paint and rubbing down in between you will get a far more resilient finish which is less likely to chip or scratch. (8, 9, 10)

vii. To finish the treatment, rub in three coats of black furniture wax and give your wood a splendid final buff. This should bring a lovely mellow sheen to your paintwork and add a little more protection from knocks. (11)

My fireside TV-watching chair at home has this paint finish on the show wood and it remains unblemished despite considerable sustained misuse.

Other Finishes

Here are the products I find most useful.

11a. Scratch cover—useful, quick remedy for bashed wood

11b. Reviver—magic potion

11c. Gray stain—easy to use, water based stain

11d. Clear wax

11e. Liming wax—for the Scandi look.

11f. Dark oak wax

Castors

The addition of a carefully chosen set of castors can transform a project. For *murder on the chaise* (pictured on page 2), I used a set of black enamel square cup castors on a new set of screw-in legs that I had painted black—they literally make my heart leap every time I see them. Underneath the ottoman that was part of the *microbia* collection lurks a set of yellow enamel castors—if they don't make your heart leap I think you need to check your pulse. (12, 13)

Fabric-covered legs

This is a useful treatment if the legs on your chair aren't very beautiful and won't improve with a paint treatment. Be sure to position the fabric seam on the inside of the leg. I usually attach the fabric with matching colored gimp pins. Always hammer a dome of silence into the bottom of the leg. All the furniture in my colorful Sri Lankan collection had fabric-covered legs; *chameleon* (p144), *gecko, elephant*. (14, 15)

THE FRAME

Gray stain

For this treatment I sanded off the old varnish and applied a coat of dilute gray stain on a clean cloth. When it was dry, I rubbed it down with fine wire wool until a little of the grain was visible. Then I used clear wax polish to finish. (16)

Liming wax

I used liming wax to get a pale Scandi look on this fluffy white chair. The midsection of the arm was made from a darker wood, so I used a very dilute gray stain under the liming wax on that section. (17)

Metal finishes

Metal cladding part or all of a frame can be an effective treatment. The A4 (8.3 x 11.7in/21 x 30cm) aluminum embossing sheets that I use are widely available online and come in a variety of colors. It's very malleable and easy to cut with scissors. I simply hammered the metal to the wood using small domed-headed nails—3/0 x 10mm/ nickel on steel nails.

Here, painted with black metal paint, rubbed back with wire wool, and waxed. (18)

Distressed and rubbed over with black paint. (19, 20)

Copper-colored aluminum sheets. (21)

New legs for old

Sometimes the legs on a chair are so ugly that they have to go! It's less dramatic than you might think to saw the legs off a chair—provided what you are left with forms a strong enough base for a screw-in replacement.

An example of this is *do the math*. I replaced the Queen Anne style legs at the front of the chair with a new pair of square screw-in legs. I simply stained and wax-polished the new legs to match the back legs. (22, 23)

Reviver

Reviver does exactly what its name suggests: cleans and revives old, dirty wood before waxing. It feeds and restores a frame beautifully. It contains oil, so don't use it before a paint treatment. I've been mixing up the same reviver for thirty years—you'd think I'd know it by heart, but I still have to check my old recipe every time! (24)

Recipe: equal parts of
• white spirit
• boiled linseed oil
• white vinegar
• methylated spirits—a dash

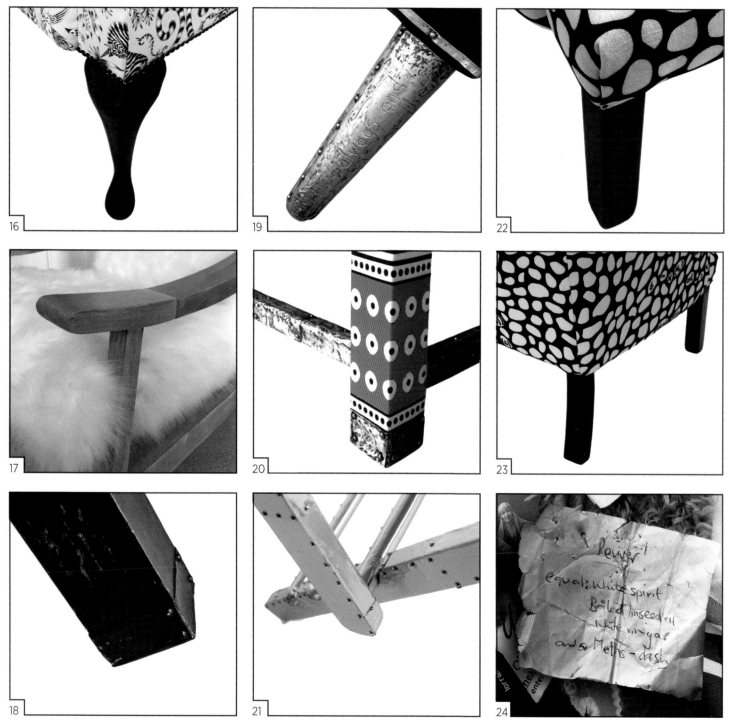

16

19

22

17

20

23

18

21

24

the guts

Let's talk upholstery.

First of all, I think it's time I laid out my credentials. I began my training back in 1986 at the London College of Furniture in the East End of London. It was a glorious place: an office block completely dedicated to woodworking and the allied trades such as instrument making, cabinet making, and French polishing.

We were taught all aspects of traditional and modern upholstery, as well as carpentry, wood finishing, and soft furnishing—often tutored by the old boys who had written the definitive guide to their trade. Now I can appreciate how lucky I was to get such a comprehensive, first-rate training.

By the time I left (clutching my City & Guilds Certificate) the college already had plans to move away from the traditional trades in favor of design courses; today the place is unrecognizable.

In those days we also had the unimaginable luxury of a full discretionary grant. By dint of working nights throughout my time as a student, I was able to save all that lovely free money to set up my first workshop in an old piano factory in Wandsworth. I was in business and have never had a day's unemployment since. I spent the first part of my career in London working for antique dealers, furniture restorers, and interior designers—almost exclusively on antiques. I've certainly served my time with the scrim and the horsehair.

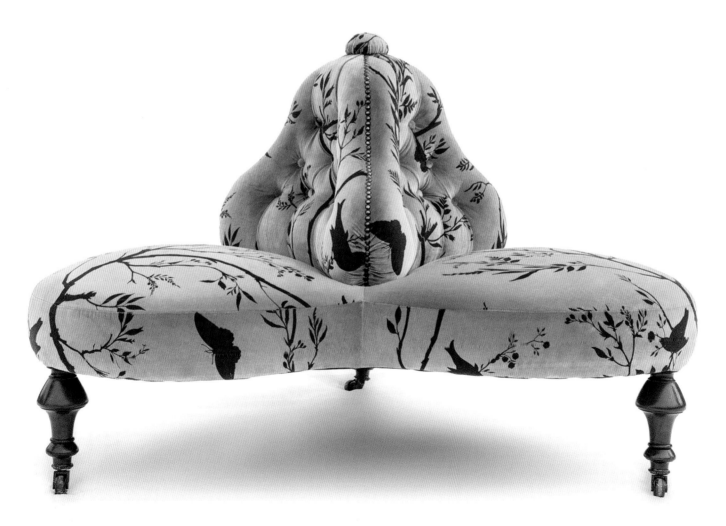

THE GUTS
materials

Traditional vs. Modern

Can we have a word about upholstery snobs? As a modern upholsterer with a traditional training I have a foot in both camps, so I find the snobbery that exists between the two rather amusing. I've known upholsterers who literally regard foam as the devil's spawn.

I would agree that valuable antique furniture should be approached with a gentle hand and reupholstered using comparable, sympathetic materials and traditional techniques—that's restoration. There's no gray area there.

But a chair that is already in a skip is very unlikely to be a priceless antique (trust me), so if you are prepared to throw it a lifeline, then go ahead and replace traditional materials with modern. It makes sense. Especially if you are hoping to sell your renovations. The furniture-buying public rarely appreciate the labor that goes into traditional work and are not often prepared to pay for it.

I have one more point to make on the subject of appropriate materials, which is best illustrated by this curious story. I once had a client with a valuable antique chaise longue that sat in pride of place in their beautiful home. They were very keen to have it reupholstered traditionally by a professional who would restore it to its original Victorian splendor. Quite right, too.

I didn't have the heart to tell them that when I opened up the seat, what I found inside was a pile of rubbish that contained, among other things, a dressing gown, a pair of kitchen curtains, and a very, very old telephone directory. This is obviously a bizarre and extreme case of using whatever materials came to hand, but it demonstrates the point I'm making; upholsterers throughout history have always used what is available to them to do the job.

In 1720 it was straw and nails, in 1820 it was horsehair and tacks, and in 2020 it's foam and staples.

Stock Materials

I run a pretty tight ship in my workshop. These are the materials I always have in stock and use every day (see photo opposite):

1a. Webbing—jute, 12lb (5.4kg)
1b. Tarpaulin—16oz (453.5gm)/heavy hessian—12oz (340gm)
1c. Scrim—10oz (283.5gm). Good for gluing over damaged upholstery.
1d. Calico—sixty strands per 1in (2.5cm) warp and weft
1e. Polyester—2oz (56 gm)
1f. Black base cloth—sixty strands per 1in (2.5cm) warp and weft
1g. 10 imp tacks—temporary tacks
1h. 10 fine tacks—for attaching the black base cloth
1i. Staples—4in (10cm)
1j. Spray adhesive—heavy duty
1k. A sheet of 0.6in (1.5cm) blue (firm seating) foam—basic remodeling foam
1l. A sheet 1in (2.5cm) blue (firm seating) foam—occasionally I have this in stock as well

I also stock these materials but use them less often (see photo opposite):

2a. Continuous zipper—black
2b. Continuous zipper—beige
2c. Laid cord—stout upholstery cord for lashing springs, but has lots of other uses
2d. Linen twine—good for sewing up hessian, and I also use it as buttoning twine
2e. Bias binding—to finish the seams on removable cushion covers
2f. Black gimp pins—for attaching outside backs and arms
2g. Back tack strips—a useful heavy cardboard strip for back-tacking outside panels

Recycle and Pass On

The most important stuff that I use everyday is not on either of my stock lists. It is the reclaimed and recycled materials that I carefully salvage and use again.

For the purpose of clearly explaining my techniques for this book, I have used new foam, calico, and polyester in my photos, just to make the illustrations clearer. Where I have explained that I glued four layers of 0.6in (1.5cm) foam together, in reality what that means is I have glued together whatever mismatched, old bits of salvaged foam I have found lying around in my store—as long as they end up 5.9in (15cm) high, I'm happy. Recycle, upcycle, renovate: call it what you like, as upholsterers it's our job to make beautiful, valuable furniture from whatever has been written off and discarded. And the more of the guts we reuse, the sweeter the job.

As I said at the beginning of this chapter, my training may have begun in 1986 but it's still ongoing—every day's a school day. The steepest learning curve for me was when I became a teacher myself and ran my own upholstery classes for ten years—in equal measure a terrifying and gratifying experience. When I look back on those years, what pleases me the most is the thought of all the hundreds and hundreds of pieces of furniture that we rescued and gave a new lease on life. We were like an army of recyclers! It also gave me the chance to pass on my trade to dozens and dozens of students: in particular, my traditional upholstery skills. I'm proud of that too.

tools

Hand Tools

I've had the same basic tool kit for over thirty-five years—with the exception of my cabriole hammer which my dad gave me thirty-eight years ago on my twenty-first birthday. I hope that illustrates the wisdom of buying the best tools you can afford—once. See photo opposite:

3a. Webbing stretcher

3b. Mallet

3c. Meter rule

3d. Soft tape measure

3e. Pliers—these are the best pair of pliers in the whole world and they're mine

3f. Cabriole hammer—narrow-headed for hammering near show wood

3g. Upholsterer's hammer—magnetic for picking-up tacks with your hammer (I don't)

3h. London ripping chisel—for lifting tacks

3i. Regulator—for lifting staples, among other uses

3j. Foam-cutting knife—Granddad's

3k. Skewers—just like giant pins, useful for pinning back layers of upholstery

3l. Ballpoint pen—for drawing on calico and fabric

3m. Marker pen—for drawing on foam

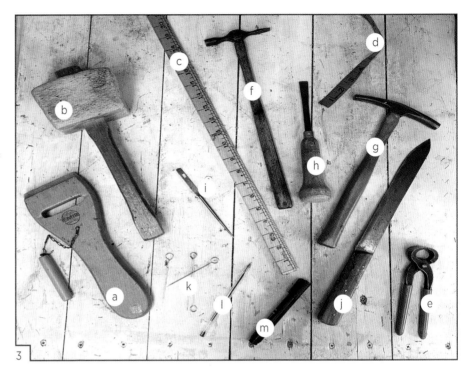

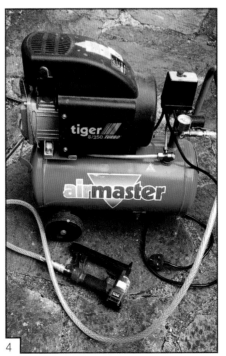

Equipment

I use a Tiger 8/250/230v ~ 50Hz compressor and a Clarke Air Stapler CS91C that uses 71/10mm staples.

The first compressor and staple gun that I bought back in the 1980s was an expensive bit of kit that only a professional would buy. However, like most manufactured goods, the prices have reduced radically. If you have the space and are serious about your projects I would recommend that you get one—it will literally change your life. No kidding. (4)

The Singer 15K sewing machine that I have used every day of my working life was given to me by my nan when I was about twelve years old. I recently had to track down a replacement for the treadle, but apart from that it has all its original parts. When I taught upholstery, I had to have several modern sewing machines in the workshop to keep everyone occupied. They were the bane of my life, perpetually going wrong and in need of constant maintenance. I thought of them as skittish, highly strung racehorses and my nan's ancient Singer as a steady old carthorse. (5)

The last bit of equipment I will mention is equally low tech. An MDF (medium density fiberboard) offcut covered with a layer of curtain interlining and a layer of calico, and a regular domestic iron. My moveable ironing station. (6)

Before we leave the subject of tools and equipment, I ought to mention the jewel in the crown of my operations—my dinky, semisubterranean workshop. When I taught upholstery, I had a huge workshop with several storerooms and a car park. Since I downsized and moved back home, my workspace may measure only 10 x 13ft (3 x 4m) but I wouldn't swap it for the world. Located a mere twenty-second commute from my front door, it's my happy place. (7)

6

7

techniques

As I said in my introduction, this book is not a step-by-step guide to upholstery. Explaining how to nail a strip of webbing to a frame and stretch it to the other side of the chair is just going over ground that has been covered a hundred times already. If you are an absolute beginner, the basic techniques of upholstery are out there on YouTube and in countless publications.

Upholstery: A Practical Guide by Desmond Gaston is the one and only book on the shelf in my workshop. I was given my copy in 1986 when I started college and I still find it useful from time to time.

That said, there are two principal techniques that I set out to explain with the furniture projects in *the stuff*: how to remodel a chair by using foam and a few other simple materials. (8)

And how to make a calico template of a chair to use as a pattern to cut the top fabric (9)

Both of these techniques are covered extensively in *lovely ovaries, drawing blood,* and *catfish.*

This leaves one final and very important set of techniques that I have so far whistled through without explanation—the dreaded cuts. I'm talking about those tricky little snips that allow the fabric to sit neatly around the frame. Nothing strikes more fear into the heart of an upholstery student than having to cut their expensive fabric to get it past a chair leg or arm. The following are a couple of cuts that you will definitely encounter.

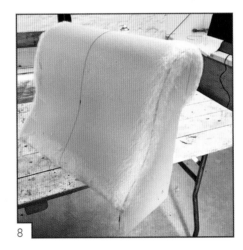

8

9

Cutting a Front Leg

Start by attaching the fabric under the rail on both sides of the leg with temporary tacks. Pull the fabric tight over the right-hand edge of the leg (where it meets the rail) and mark that point with a pin. Make the first cut to the pin. (10)

Pull the fabric firmly across to the left-hand side of the leg and temporary-tack. Trim the fabric ready for tucking up. (11)

Knock out the temporary tack, tuck up the fabric, and temporary-tack again with two tacks along the line of the fold. (12)

Now make a fold in the fabric and bring the fold to the center of the leg. Temporary-tack in place, and slip a pin along the line of the fold. (13)

Knock out the temporary tack and open up the fold. Hammer home the two tacks under the fold. Using the pin as a guide, cut a square of fabric out of the fold. This is called "cleaning out." The pin will stop you cutting too much away. (14)

Now do the same on the left-hand side of the leg. Find the point where the leg meets the rail and put in a pin. Cut to the pin. (15, 16)

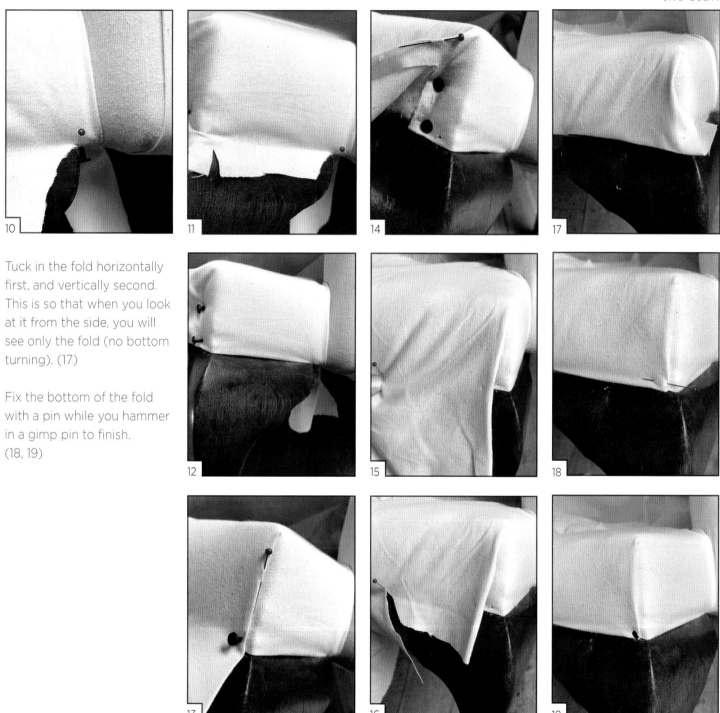

Tuck in the fold horizontally first, and vertically second. This is so that when you look at it from the side, you will see only the fold (no bottom turning). (17)

Fix the bottom of the fold with a pin while you hammer in a gimp pin to finish. (18, 19)

Cutting a Back Leg

Start by attaching the fabric under the rail on
both sides of the leg with temporary tacks.
Place a pin where the left-hand side of the
leg meets the rail. Cut to the pin. (20)

Tuck up the fabric and permanently tack the
fabric under the fold. (21)

Now do the same to the back of the leg.
Anchor the outside back fabric. Find the
place where the right-hand side of the leg
meets the rail and place a pin. Cut to the pin.
(22)

First, tuck up the horizontal edge of the fold,
then tuck in the vertical edge of the fold.
Hold in place with a pin, then hammer in a
gimp pin to finish. (23)

I hope this chapter has demonstrated that
you don't need a big, fancy workshop filled
with expensive equipment and materials to
produce good work. You already own the
most valuable resource you will ever need:
that's your imagination.

20

23

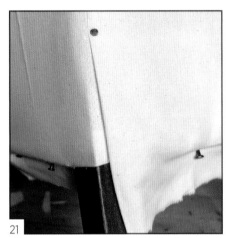

21

22

the fabric

THE FABRIC

10. Flip/Duplicate

It's useful to be able to manipulate an image. Click on Image/ Image rotation to flip and rotate an image. To duplicate a layer, simply right click on the layer you want to duplicate and click on Duplicate layer from the drop down box.

11. Merge/Flatten layers

Click on Layers and select Merge layers or Flatten image from the drop down list. Flattening an image will merge all the layers into one background layer. This is probably what you will need to do to your artwork before sending it to the online fabric printers (check with your printer first). Merge visible allows you to merge selected layers and keep others separate by clicking off the "eye" so they are not visible.

12. Offset

The Offset allows you to create a seamless piece of artwork that can be uploaded as a repeatable fabric. I'll illustrate this with my *catfish* artwork. The fish image was already repeatable vertically; here I will show you how to make it repeatable horizontally, too.

- Click on Filter/Other/Offset/Wrap around. (2)
- Move the Horizontal cursor until the "bad" join is in the middle. (3)
- Using the digital pen, redraw the image so that it repeats seamlessly. (4)

13. Shadow

This is my second favorite thing. I've explained the process in the *I'm Not Here!* fabric exercise.

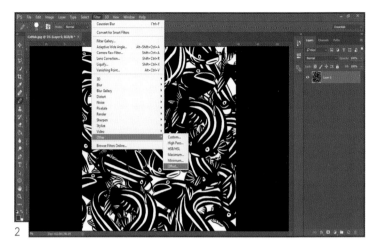

2

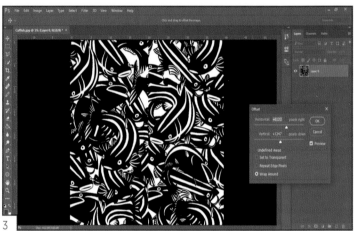

3

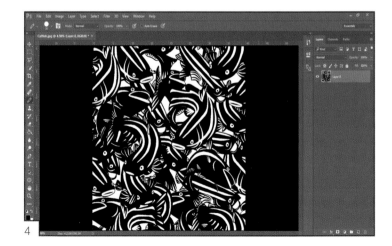

4

maintain aspect ratio ──

5

14. Maintain aspect ratio

This is a very useful little tool that will appear under the toolbar when you are using the Move tool. When you move an image it can easily become distorted: the Maintain aspect ratio will pop it back to its original shape. (5)

15. Crop tool

This is a tool you may already be familiar with from your phone. It crops away some of the background from an image, or it can crop the canvas to fit the image.

6

I'm Not Here! fabric exercise

To illustrate the use of some of these Photoshop tools I'm going to take you through the process of making a simple fabric design from beginning to end. I chose as my subject the green retro phone that sits in my office. Generally speaking, I dislike the telephone so much that when it rings, I shout, "I'm not here!"

Photoshop

I began by taking a photo of the telephone using the camera on my iPhone and downloading it to my laptop. (6)

In Photoshop I clicked Open. Found the photograph of the telephone and clicked Open again. (7)

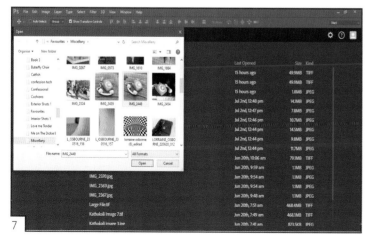

7

THE FABRIC

I had to crop the telephone from its background by using the Pen tool. Once I had traced a line of dots around the shape of the phone, I had to close the path. I clicked on Path/Load path as a Selection. Then I had to select the telephone by clicking on Select/Inverse. Finally, I switched to the Move tool, ready to drag the phone to a new canvas. I made a new canvas sized 11.8in x 11.8in (30 x 30cm)/1772 x1772px/150dpi and called it *I'm Not Here*. I dragged the telephone onto the new canvas. (8)

Then I enhanced the colors on the telephone image. I first clicked on the Set foreground color tool and used the Eyedropper and Color picker to select the color black. Then, using the Paint pot tool, I clicked on the numbers on the dial and other black features with 100% opacity black.

I lightened the color of the phone by first sampling the original green with the Eyedropper tool, then choosing a shade brighter from the Color picker. Then I used the Paint pot tool at 25% opacity to intensify the color of the telephone. Now the phone looks sharper and more vibrant. (9)

Next I put a shadow under the telephone. I pressed Ctrl + J to make a copy of the phone layer. Then I clicked on the Move tool. A rectangle appeared around the telephone; I pressed Ctrl and clicked on the center top of the rectangle. Then I dragged and warped the telephone sideways to look like a shadow. (10)

Select
Move tool
New canvas
Path
Load path as a selection
Pen tool

8

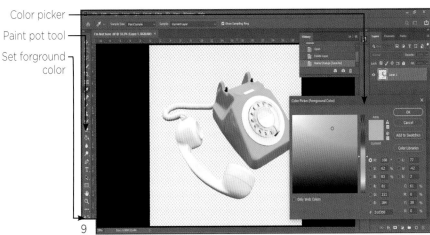

Color picker
Paint pot tool
Set forground color

9

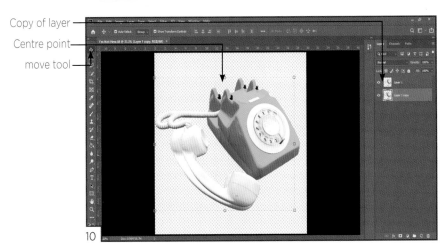

Copy of layer
Centre point
move tool

10

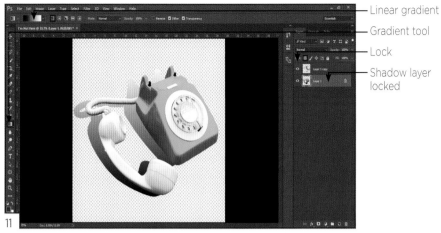

Linear gradient
Gradient tool
Lock
Shadow layer locked

I locked the "shadow" layer. Then I clicked on the Gradient tool and selected Linear Gradient/Black and White from the drop down options. I dragged a line across the warped telephone with the Gradient tool. At this point the bottom telephone turned into a gradient "shadow." (11)

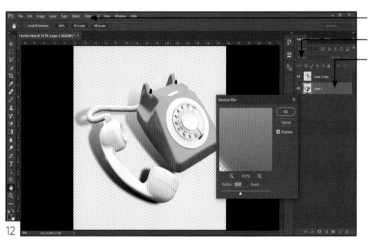

Filter
Normal Multiply
Unlocked layer

I unlocked the "shadow" layer. Then I clicked on Normal/Multiply. I went to Filter/Blur/Gaussian Blur/10 pixels. This made a deep shadow under the phone. (12)

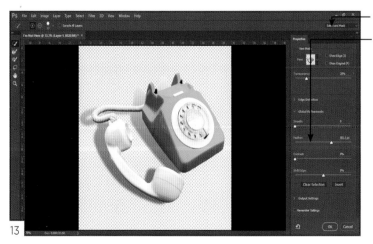

Select and mask
Feather

To blur the top of the shadow, I clicked on the Marquee tool. I dragged the Marquee tool across the top of the shadow to form a rectangle. Next I clicked on Select and Mask and from the drop-down options selected Feather/approx.100px. (13)

THE FABRIC

Still with the Marquee tool across the top of the shadow, I went to Filter/Blur/Gaussian Blur/100 pixels, which made it very blurred. (14)

Finally to complete the shadow, I went to Layers/Opacity/approx. 75%. (15)

Now that my shadow was in place, I needed a background color to finish the job. I made a new canvas sized 11.8 x 11.8in (30 x 30cm)/1772 x 1772px/150dpi. I called this canvas I'm not here fabric.

Using the Set Foreground tool and Color Picker, I chose a mesmerizing periwinkle blue and painted the new canvas with the Paint pot tool. I dragged the telephone shadow layer to the new canvas. Then I dragged the telephone layer to the new canvas and repositioned the shadow to make it look like it was floating over the periwinkle surface. (16)

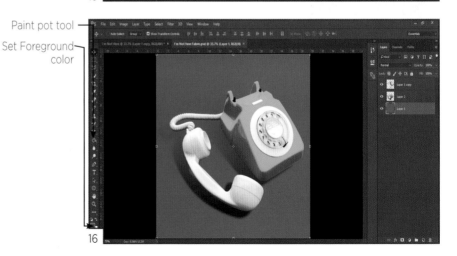

Marquee tool

Opacity

Paint pot tool

Set Foreground color

Finally, I flattened the image and saved it as I'm not here fabric.jpg ready to upload to the online printers. I decided to print my simple bright design on heavy Panama cotton, 59in (150cm) wide, and I used the Repeat Style Drop/½ to make a more interesting pattern. (17, 18)

17

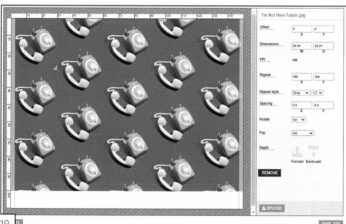

18

Fabric Choice

A large part of the design equation is choosing the right fabric. Should it be crisp, sharp cotton; grainy, organic linen; or sumptuous, tactile velvet? This is where a 4in (10cm) sample from the online printers will really help you decide which fabric suits your design. I tend to use the same four fabrics for all my designs.

Panama heavy cotton, 310g/sq m (9oz/sq yd)
A strong flat cotton fabric that prints detailed designs very clearly. *Drawing blood* is a good example of a design with loads of written information that I really wanted people to be able to read! (19)

Linen union, 349g/sq m (10.25oz/sq yd)
A grainy, more organic-looking fabric suited to vintage projects. The *1967* chair designs worked well on linen. (20)

19

20

Cotton furnishing velvet, 416g/sq m (12.25oz/sq yd)
Not so good for very detailed designs, but fantastic for bold block colors. Velvet was the only fabric that could have delivered the opulence I was aiming for with the project *she's running the country*. (21)

Satin/Sateen cotton, 230g/sq m (6.75oz/sq yd)
The lightest weight fabric I would recommend for upholstery. Satin cotton has a subtle sheen for genteel projects like *murder on the chaise*. (22, 23)

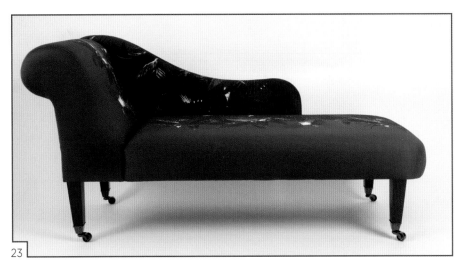

printing

I'd like to begin by emphasizing once again that I am not a digital printer, I'm a customer: I rely on the technical expertise of an online printer to turn my artwork into fabric. So the most important thing is that you find a good, reliable printer who can advise you and help with your projects. I've used three online printers over the years, and I can honestly say that quality varies. You'll have to shop around like I did to find a service that delivers what you want. I eventually found my dream team at the Center for Advanced Textiles at Glasgow School of Art. (24)

The staff at Glasgow, led by Alan Shaw, offers a terrific online service and their work is consistently good. If I upload a piece of artwork that isn't quite right, the team at Cat Digital won't just go ahead and print the error—they get in touch and discuss the problem. They've saved me from myself on many occasions.

It's not as expensive as you might think either; in fact I'd say it cost decidedly less than a lot of upholstery fabrics per yard/meter from conventional outlets.

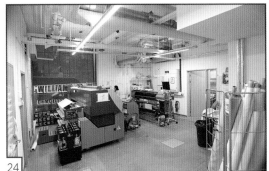

Uploading Artwork to Be Printed

Once you've poured your artistic soul into an incredible piece of artwork, what next? In reality it's not possible to offer a definitive answer that applies to all print jobs. Requirements may vary from one online printer to another, and it also depends on what you're trying to achieve with your design.

That said, in the interest of simplicity and accuracy, I asked Alan at Cat Digital to summarize for me what is generally required. He said, "The optimum size of a file is really dictated by the actual print size of the printed image, design, or repeat tile. Normally we would advise files are no less than 150dpi (dots per inch) at actual print size."

In short, an image less than 150dpi isn't clear enough to print, and working on a canvas that is the actual size of the fabric image makes life easier for everyone. Don't forget to flatten the image and save it as a JPEG before you upload—that may vary too!

Remember, your job is to design—the printer's job is to print. If you have a problem or a question about the file you want to upload, simply ask. At the back end of most online print websites are teams of knowledgeable people who should be happy to help. If they're not—try another website.

Digital Textile Printing Is Greener!

In comparison to the traditional print process, digital textile printing can be considered a more sustainable and eco-friendly alternative. Actual screen production is not required and this eliminates a lot of cost, time, and chemicals, before a job can even begin. Since the digital process uses only the ink required for the job, there is very little ink wasted at point of print, and also at the wash off stage, since less water and energy are required.

A further development is the pigment printer. The *catfish* design was printed this way and I was delighted with the fabric. The pigment printer uses dry heat to fix the dyes after printing; no washing is necessary, and so less water is wasted. The process also allows for previously printed fabrics to be reused since the pigment ink sits happily on top of what is already there. (25)

Recycling printed fabric—how brilliant is that?

25

Printing Top Tip

Finally, I asked Alan Shaw from Cat Digital for his printing top tip.

"I think my top tip would be always to sample a print before committing to a longer run. Certain prints or dye types will always suit one base cloth more than another, so a sample will help identify the correct process and save time and money in the long run."

I agree with Alan.

THE FABRIC
quantifying

The method for quantifying fabric is the same for all chairs, large or small (or round!).

There are quite a few Parker Knoll fireside chairs in the book, so I thought it was an obvious choice to demonstrate the process.

Using a soft tape, measure and list the horizontal and vertical dimensions of every panel on the chair (plus generous turnings of approximately 1.9in (5cm)). It's useful to add an arrow indicating which are the horizontal measurements (in case they get mixed up and placed on the fabric the wrong way round). (26)

Draw a rectangle on a sheet of paper to represent the fabric lying on a table. Then, draw an approximate outline of each pattern piece from the measurements; fitting them as neatly and efficiently as you can within the width of the fabric (which is 55in/1.40cm).

You may also have to consider where the design will appear on each pattern piece. As with this illustration, there is a linear motif that must be centered on each pattern piece. To work out the fabric estimate, simply add up all the measurements on the left-hand side of the "fabric"—which, in the case of this chair, comes to 5.9ft (1.80cm). It's a good idea to round-up to the nearest full meter. The fabric estimate for this chair is 6.5ft (2m) of 55in (1.40cm) wide linen union. (27)

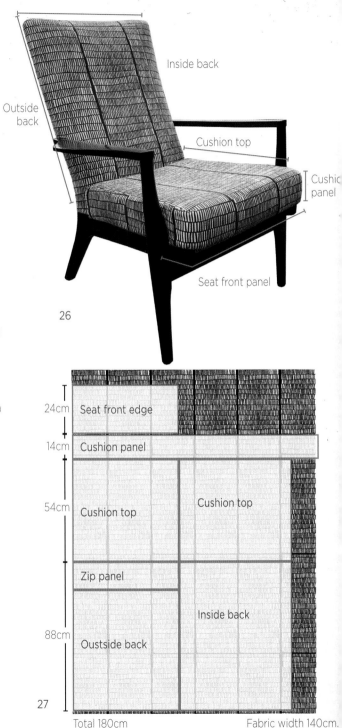

Inside back:	34.6 x 25.6in (88 x 65cm) >
Outside back:	27.5 x 22.8in (70 x 58cm) >
Cushion top:	21 x 22in (54 x 56cm) >
Seat front panel:	9.5 x 19.7in (24 x 50cm) >
Zip panel:	6 x 20in (16 x 51cm) >
Cushion panel:	5.5 (14cm) x the width

the wrinkles

trims

To be honest, I don't use a lot of trimmings on my own work. That could be because I started my career in the frilly 1980s, when everything was so festooned with buttons, bows, and bullion, that it permanently blew out my trimmings circuit. Ornate braids and tassels may not do it for me, but I love to see them on other people's work, and when I taught upholstery we would happily spend hours discussing the merits of one ruche fringe over another—heaven.

Here are a few of the simple trimmings and finishing touches I use.

Characterful spring coverings
Not strictly speaking a trimming, but a final flourish nonetheless. A quilted silk spring cover luxuriating under a box cushion is always a welcome sight. (1)

Close nails
Close nails or domed-headed nails are my favorite trimming. (2–6)

Gimp pins
I use black-headed gimp pins on most of my projects, but occasionally the job calls for a colored pin. Because nail varnish is quite durable and comes in masses of silly colors, it's perfect for painting the head of a gimp pin to match a fabric. (7, 8)

Metal trim
This is definitely my kind of trimming: a no-nonsense metal strip nailed to a chair. Job done. (9)

1

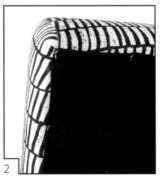
4

7

2

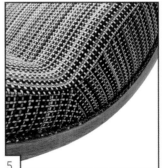
5

8

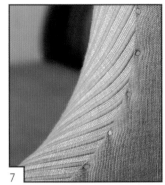
3

6

9

tips

Here are a dozen of my top tips.

1. Gimp pins have a tendency to buckle and corkscrew when hammered into a hardwood frame. A couple of whacks with a mallet on a regulator will pilot out a hole—then you can hammer the gimp pin home without bending it.

2. Collect old socks and use them to protect your beautiful polished chair legs from the rough and tumble of the workshop. Pull them on and fix them at the top of the leg with tightly bound masking tape.

3. When preparing a piece of foam for deep buttoning, a short length of copper pipe (about 4.7in/12cm long) sharpened at one end with a metal file will cut a perfect hole through a piece of foam.

4. To deal with fraying threads when you have made a cut in your top fabric (to get around a leg or arm), smear a little Copydex glue on the wrong side of the fabric (at the point of the cut) and press all the fraying strands onto the glue.

5. Self-cover buttons aren't very robust in my opinion. To strengthen them, first cover the front of the button with the fabric as normal, then fill the back of the button with glue from a hot glue gun before clicking the metal back cover into place. You end up with a solid near indestructible button. (10)

6. When buttoning a patterned fabric, it's well worth going the extra mile and pattern matching the covered buttons. (11)

7. If you have a decent pair of sharp scissors for cutting fabric never use then on webbing or hessian: that's the quickest way to blunt them.

8. To get a perfect bond when gluing foam together, generously spray adhesive on both surfaces and wait for six minutes before you bring the glued surfaces together. Not five, not seven, but six.

9. Calico is a loomstate cloth, which means it is sold as it comes off the loom; it isn't pressed or finished like normal fabric. To cut out a straight (true) piece of calico you have to measure out what you want, snip with the scissors and tear the fabric along the grain. It won't look straight, but it will be true.

10. I always have a 6in (16cm) regulator in my tool kit. A short, fat regulator is almost unbreakable regardless of how you abuse it—unlike longer regulators, which tend to snap at the end.

11. When you have finished stripping the old upholstery from a frame, fill the tack holes and any other minor damage with "porridge." Porridge is made from roughly equal parts of fine sawdust and wood glue. It's not only cheap and fairly non-toxic, it works sympathetically with the wood. Some modern wood fillers dry harder than the wood itself and can literally shatter when stapled or tacked.

12. When I finish a chair I always make at least one scatter cushion from the remaining fabric. They retail separately in the gallery where I sell my work, but if someone is interested in the chair, the gallery owner can throw in the cushion for free, and, it is hoped, make the sale. Which brings me neatly to the next subject . . .

selling

Now that you've created an outstanding collection of furniture, you might be hoping to sell some of it. Let me share with you what I have learned on the subject.

The Gallery

Currently, I sell all my work through an art gallery in my home town of Totnes. It's a busy place in the center of town called the bowie gallery, which is owned and run by Annie Bowie. Annie is a passionate, knowledgeable gallerist with a large client base and a gift for putting people and art together.

There are obvious advantages to selling this way; having my stuff on display in an uncluttered gallery setting emphasizes its uniqueness and adds a certain cachet: not to mention value. (12)

Also, I invest my work with ideas and opinions; when Annie sells one of my pieces in the gallery, the client buys into this and takes the story away too. (13)

Over time, my work has gained equal billing with the artists who exhibit at the gallery and Annie has helped establish my name as a respected maker of bonkers furniture. I'm happy with that. (14)

This is how it works: I deliver a piece of furniture to the gallery, and Annie sells it and, if necessary, ships it. I get paid.

Generally a gallery will take between 40% and 50% in commission. Of course this is much higher than online selling sites, but the packing and shipping is taken care of, and the gallery offers my work a clear space to be appreciated in an extremely overcrowded marketplace. On balance, I would prefer to spend more time in the workshop making furniture than focusing on keyword optimization or my click through rate.

12

13

14

The Online Selling Platform

As well as good old eBay and Etsy, there are a number of very good online selling platforms for furniture and they take a small commission compared to a gallery. Personally, I have never had much luck with any of them. Either my furniture didn't sell at all, or in order to sell it, I had to let it go too cheaply. I also found that packing and shipping chairs and sofas from my home in Devon was expensive and could be fraught with difficulties.

Just because I haven't found these sites to be a good fit for my work, that doesn't mean they won't work for you. Try them for yourself.

One final observation I would like to make about crowded online selling platforms. I find that when I pitch my work into a sea of stylish conventional furniture it makes my stuff look mad . . . but not in a good way!

The Selling Website

A few years ago I set up a website with the intention to sell all my work through my own online shop. The website cost a stupid amount of money to set up and took forever to get right—about a year in fact. When it was finally up and running, I realized that unless I spent a large chunk of my time directing people to the site (or paying someone else to do it) I wasn't going to have any customers. And I didn't. I can't say I regret the whole exercise. What I have is an extremely expensive but very flashy online showcase for my work, which has paid dividends in other ways. Not least, in the commissioning of this book.

These days, if you're in business you need some sort of online presence; we all know that.

Keep it simple and stylish is my advice—but doesn't that apply to everything in life?

www.lorraine-osborne.co.uk

175

glossary and acknowledgments

anchoring pins
Pins that are not forming the seams of a pattern, but holding the cloth in place on the chair

chamfered edge
The edge of any material with a depth that has been cut on the diagonal to reduce its bulk

dome of silence
A small, pronged metal dome that is hammered into the bottom of a chair leg as a glider

dpi
Dots per inch

home
To staple or tack permanently to a frame

inside back and inside arms
The three sections of the chair that meet the seat

JPEG/jpg
Joint Photographic Experts Group. Saving finished artwork as a .jpg compresses it to one background layer

lumber swell/region
A gentle swell of upholstery that supports the lower spine when seated in an armchair

mirror image
Transferring the shape from one side of a pattern piece to the other

notch
A tiny triangular cut through both layers of a seam for the purpose of reassembling both layers of the seam in the same place/ or for marking the center of a piece of cloth

offer up
To try something out on a chair before sewing/gluing/cutting, etc

outside back and outside arms
The three outside sections of a chair

Photoshop
Design program software

platform seat
A seat with a flat construction designed to have a separate cushion

px
Pixel

shoddy
Salvaged wool/mixed felt

stuff over seat
An upholstered seat without a cushion

template
A three-dimensional pattern made by pinning calico pieces to a seat/inside arm/ inside back, etc

temporary-tack
To part-hammer a tack that has been into a frame to hold a layer of cloth temporarily

TIFF/tif
Tagged Image File Format. Artwork in progress can be saved as a .tif to keep the layers separate and avoid compression and loss of clarity

top cover
Fabric

I'd like to thank a few people and acknowledge their contribution to the book:

Alan Shaw at the Centre for Advanced Textiles at Glasgow School of Art for patiently checking my facts.
www.catdigital.co.uk

Annie Bowie at the bowie gallery for her faith and enthusiasm.
www.thebowiegallery.co.uk

All my ex-upholstery students for teaching me so much about upholstery.
Especially Gina Carter; the original Arse Artist.